WALKING ON AIRE

Walking On Aire

my quest for adventure along
Yorkshire's 'exotic' river

Andy Owens

4ward Books

First Published in the United Kingdom in 2010 by

4Ward Books
P.O. Box 714
Halifax
HX1 9NA

Walking On Aire
Copyright © Andy Owens, 2010

ISBN: 978-0-9565696-0-8

A catalogue record exists for this book in the British Library

Cover Cartoon: Mike Bryson www.drawnbymike.com
Cover Design: Mike Barret frogsdesign

Printed and bound in England by Booksprint

Dedication

For Mom and Dad and David
With all my love and thanks

Acknowledgements

Although this is my eighth book, it is also my first self-published book, and I would like to thank various people for advice and help, including fellow self-published authors John Billingsley and Jill Robinson, plus Chris Ratcliffe of Pennine Pens, Laighton Waymouth of Booksprint, Mark Reid of the 'Innway' guides, Siobhan Curham for her self-publishing column in *Writers' Forum* magazine and the new magazine *Publish Now!* The biggest thank you goes to my best friend Silvie Haller for lending me money towards the printing so I could push ahead with the book!

Most of the books about explorers which I found helpful are mentioned in the text. The ones not included are *Explorers* (BBC Books, 1975) by Desmond Wilcox; *Teacup in a Storm* (Collins, 2005) by Mick Conefrey, and *Traversa* (Duckworth, 2007) by Fran Sandham.

Indirect thanks to a variety of writers who have influenced my own work over the years, including Douglas Adams, Bill Bryson, Wendy Cope, Agatha Christie, Josie Dew, David Lodge, Ian McMillan, Jonathan Meades, Peter Mortimer, Joe Orton and, particularly, Mark Wallington, who wrote several books, including the brilliant *Boogie Up The River* – which first inspired me to become a writer.

Chapter One

My 40th birthday had long since gone and if life didn't begin soon, I was going to demand a refund.

Whilst others my age had realised that life was already at least halfway through, and so were off snowboarding or skydiving or mountaineering or yachting around the world and making the most of it, I felt left behind, cautiously tackling the brow of middle-age, slipping and sliding down the other side, gamely struggling with whatever life was amused to throw at me next.

Life – and all its best bits – seemed to be wilfully avoiding me. Fun and Excitement played practical jokes on me, then waved smugly from afar. Love and Romance gave me the slip, pouting and giggling, running off together, hand in hand, into the sunset. Mystery and Intrigue, dressed in dark glasses and trench coats, left a trail of red herrings, then slinked into the shadows.

But then Life doesn't knock on doors. It doesn't cold-call. Bearing gifts of golden nuggets on silver platters. I had to make an effort. Do something simply outstanding. Something I could brag about. Show off with at parties. Wax lyrical about to future fans. Use as a substitute for crap chat-up lines.

I had often considered packing a rucksack and setting off into the wide blue yonder over the hill and far away, with no agenda, no schedule, no deadlines, to move with the flow of the wind, and go wherever the feeling took me. But I could end up walking round in circles. Ambling or dawdling can get you nowhere fast.

What I needed was a specific route and destination. As the renowned walker and writer Alfred Wainwright, wrote: 'One should always have a definite objective. In a walk, as in life, it is so much more satisfying to reach a target by personal effort than to wander aimlessly. An objective is an ambition – and life without ambition is, well, aimless wandering.'

Plus, I was a writer without a story. So that's what I needed. A story. But a *real* one. A series of situations in which to place myself. Just like some of my favourite writers and their books: Mark Wallington, *Boogie up the River*. Bill Bryson, *A Walk in the Woods*. Peter Mortimer, *Broke Through Britain*. Writers who travel rather than travel writers. All quite different. All quite brilliant. And my *own* plan? I would take a rucksack and notebook, with no prior research, and just see what happened. See what occurred to me. If anything.

I remember standing in the shower one day, mulling over the possibilities, watching all the water splash down the drain, when I suddenly – mysteriously – felt an urge to walk the length of a great river.

Colourful and exotic images whizzed through my mind: the Congo, Ganges, Nile and Amazon. I had always been enthralled by accounts of the great explorers and wanted some of that excitement and glory for myself.

Baron Humboldt, an early explorer of South America, wrote: 'From earliest youth I had dreamt longingly of travelling in faraway countries, rarely visited by Europeans. Even as a child, the sight of exotic trees, foreign maps and descriptions of tropic Zones, had been enough to move me to tears. The yearning of my childhood was indeed a longing for a homeland for my soul.'

I began reading accounts of explorers, on their journeys in faraway lands, trekking across deserts, through jungles, up rivers, and I planned to follow in their footsteps. More rashly, I announced my intention to family and friends, colleagues at work, sometimes total strangers I accosted in the street.

But then came the bombshell.

Whichever exotic river I chose, there would be exotic creatures, too. Fierce creatures, with scary teeth. How would a person – who had never ventured further north than Inverness, or further south than Calais – survive in the wild and dangerous places where lions, tigers, apes, snakes and crocodiles attack each other – and anything else which is naïve enough to wander into their territory – with alarming frequency and ferocity? The closest I had ever come to an ape was watching *King Kong*, and the nearest I had been to a tiger was on a box of Frosties.

I had seen various wild animals close-up as a child, on a family trip to Knowlsley Safari Park. As my Dad drove us there, we arrived with high hopes and left with a high pile of baboon bob on the bonnet. But that was the limit of my experience with ferocious beasties. What was the point of marking my forty-first year with an expedition so dangerous that it may ensure I would never see my forty-second?

Besides, my last book was called *Paranormal West Yorkshire* and during the research I had been spooked by ghosts, buzzed by UFOs, abducted by aliens, stalked by Mystery

Big Cats, had my fingers burnt by Spontaneous Human Combustion and played hide & seek with the Cottingley Fairies. The last thing I needed was another fright.

African explorer Mary Kingsley was near suicidal following the death of her parents, so she thought of an endeavour so dangerous, that she might get herself killed by attempting it! In her book, *Travels in West Africa* (1897), she wrote: 'In 1893 (aged 31), for the first time in my life, I found myself in possession of 5 or 6 months which were not heavily forestalled and, feeling like a boy with a new half-crown, I lay about in my mind… as to what to do with them.' Mary decided to travel to West Africa. Her friends tried to dissuade her. It was the White Man's Grave, they told her. It was inhabited by head-hunters. A woman hadn't a chance of survival. Which appealed to her in a morbid way. So she went – and survived. And the reason she survived? She was a thoroughly tough cookie. She wrote of an encounter with a crocodile, 'who chose to get his paws over the stern of my canoe,' to which Mary had to 'retire to the bows and fetch him a clip on the snout with a paddle.'

However, Mary was undoubtedly made of sterner stuff than myself, so I took a reality check and plumped for something less exotic and a little closer to home. Yorkshire had its great rivers too. After all, who needs killer crocs and head-shrinking cannibals to complete a trip? I thought it pretty unlikely I would have to wrestle bears like Daniel Boone, or lions and tigers like Tarzan. But who knows what could happen? A local river may not be uncharted territory for mankind in general. But it was to *me*. All sorts of perils could lay in wait to ambush the next intrepid expeditionary.

I spread my map out on the floor and scoured the county

for little blue lines. The thick lines were canals, the thinner ones rivers. And they were all there. The Ouse, Esk, Ure, Calder, Wharfe, Derwent, Swale and Aire.

As a writer, always on the lookout for catchy titles, the Aire sprang out at me like a grasshopper on speed: *Walking On Aire* sounded the best. I'm good at puns. I've got an English degree.

This river probably wouldn't be a tourist's first choice. The Ouse and the others would no doubt attract most, for they were the big boys of Yorkshire rivers. The ones who had earned their place in guidebooks, gracing the pages of Beautiful Yorkshire calendars and county magazines, the darlings of tourist information centres and souvenir tea cosies, weaving their watery way through the Yorkshire Dales, and into the hearts of holidaymakers.

But countryside and picturesque locations, although beautiful, could still become monotonous. Same old, same old. I suppose I was a tourist, of sorts – but I would be travelling first and foremost as a writer. I wanted to chart the changing face of a river, with its different moods and identities. The Aire seemed to have a mixture of everything. From peaceful and tranquil, to urban and suburban. Villages, towns, even a city. Rural, residential, industrial, historical, archaeological. This particular river may not have the airs and graces of the Ouse and others, as it did not limit itself to picture-postcard destinations, though it did possess a few of its own.

Beginning in North Yorkshire, deep in the Dales, at remote Malham, it flows through a few small villages with strange names like Bell Busk and Coniston Cold, and on to market town Skipton. In West Yorkshire, it proceeds through the former industrial towns of Bingley and Keighley, and Sir Titus Salt's famous creation Saltaire, then onto Esholt, where they filmed parts of the TV series *Emmerdale*. It has distinctive features like Apperley Bridge marina and ancient Kirkstall Abbey, plus the hustle and bustle of Leeds. Moving through further suburbs, it leads to Castleford, a former coal-mining town but now with regeneration galore, before returning to North Yorkshire and villages with quaint Miss Marple-type place names like Temple Hurst and Chapel Haddesley, before finally ending at Airmyn, near Goole, in East Yorkshire.

The Aire sounded like my kind of river. And I felt the quirky title would help in some way, too. 'I'm walking the River Aire,' I would say. 'I'm writing a book about it called *Walking On Aire*.'

I would utter this wherever I went. It would be an icebreaker. A passport to pleasure. People would welcome me into their homes. Offer me unlimited hospitality. The hand of friendship. Ply me with food and drink and naughty narcotics. Beg me to marry their daughters. And the family wealth. Or maybe not.

So that was decided. What I needed now was some serious preparation.

What about some physical exercise to prepare me for what could prove to be a challenging experience? I rooted through my treasured collection of classic travel literature for a suitable mentor.

From an early age, Antarctic explorer Roald Amunsden became obsessed about his fitness. Apart from keep-fit exercises, he slept with his windows open in an effort to toughen himself. I tried this myself, caught the flu and had to postpone the expedition by a fortnight.

But his ambitions didn't simply stop there. Although he admired the great explorers, he was not the sort to simply collect autographs of his idols. He wrote: 'What appealed to me most strongly was the suffering (they had) endured. A strange ambition burned within me to share those same sufferings.'

Well, I was happy to rough it slightly once in a while, but suffering is not something that would give me pleasure. No doubt his attitude would have gone down a treat on *I'm A Celebrity – Get Me Out Of Here*, having rats crawling over his head and eating fish-eyes and stick insects and lying in baths of beetles and spiders, but despite my early admiration of Amundsen, I decided he was probably not the sort of chap I wanted as a mentor on my trip into the wilderness.

I've always liked the idea of travel. And it's not because of the desire to meet different people, perhaps concluding that we are all brethren of the collective unconscious - brothers and sisters on a journey of the long, dark tea-time of the soul in mind, space and time, connected in some deep and mysterious way to the eternal life-force – and all that New Age nonsense. It's simply because I hate being in one place for too long.

Familiarity and habit seem to ruin everything in the end. Hence another reason for my expedition. To cast off what is old and tired and familiar, and replace it with something which may not actually be different, but at least *looks* and *feels* so.

Despite his worrying desire to suffer, Roald Amundsen was much admired for how he prepared for an expedition. He tried to anticipate any situation he may encounter, and then plan for it in meticulous detail. He was orderly and neat, obsessed with logistics: 'I can do twice the amount of work when I see tidiness and comfort around me,' he wrote. 'Victory awaits him who has everything in order. Defeat is certain for him who has neglected to take the necessary precautions in time.' Amundsen wanted to 'strip exploration of its mystery', but I realised that too much preparation could be the death of a journey. I didn't want to over-plan. A little unpredictability would give an otherwise run-of-the-mill trip a refreshing zing.

Not only was he dubbed the 'best man to go exploring with', but also the 'best-dressed explorer'! Buoyed by this, I started thinking about my wardrobe. I drew the line at that ridiculous *Carry On Up The Congo / It Aint Half Hot Mum* khaki jungle get-up, but it was important to look the part. Who knows whom I might meet? I didn't want to be mistaken for some aimless weekend rambler or, worse still, some amateurish writer with nothing in particular to write about, too cowardly to explore a tropical landscape complete with fierce creatures and their scary teeth, opting instead for some little known, comparatively safe and frankly uninspiring backwater set deep in the Yorkshire landscape. So I needed to consider my appearance. Clean jeans and jacket, plus 'sensible' hiking boots should suffice.

Next morning, I awoke at a time so early that nocturnal scavengers were still on the prowl, kickboxing the dustbin and abseiling the bird-table.

I drew back the curtains and winced.

Grumpy old British winter had outstayed his welcome again. His tenancy agreement long since expired, he knew he could not resist for long. Only yesterday, as Spring nervously peeped out from under the heavy blanket of snow, the plants had begun to yawn and stretch and get back into the swing of things. February had thawed out, leaving March to mop up the mess.

Most of us awake on such mornings, with the realisation that the day is going to be much like any other. Treading the wheel of routine. The nine-to-five humdrum.

Yet today, when everyone else awakes, you will be long

gone into the yonder: rucksack bouncing, boots clomping, with an altogether different agenda.

After all, a holiday doesn't truly begin when you arrive at your destination, but on wrenching yourself from sleep, wondering who was daft enough to set the alarms so early.

The early morning routine remains much the same for everyone. Stumbling over shoes and other oddments you really should have stored away the night before. The sudden wince as the shine of the bathroom light ricochets off each wall and stings your eyes. The momentary fright as you glimpse your groggy, bleary-eyed face in the mirror, wondering what Stig-of-the-Dump is doing in your bathroom. And the high-pitched scream as a jet of icy shower spray hits you, wondering why you always twist the wrong dial when you have shampoo in your eyes.

Yet such are the ablutions of the true traveller – mundane meanderings are the prologues of adventure.

Though now it was time to cease all this pontificating and prevaricating and get on with this expedition, this adventure, this walk on the wild side – which would begin at Malham in the Yorkshire Dales.

But first I had to get there.

Chapter Two

'Is this the bus to Malham?'

Daft question, really. I was stood at the Malham bus stop, next to a bus with the word Malham slapped on the front, and a fed-up looking driver wearing a cap with a 'If you ain't been to Malham, you ain't been Nowhere,' sticker stuck to it. He had the resigned expression of a man doomed to a career of answering dopey questions. So he sighed, nodded and forced a smile.

'Malham, yes. This is the bus to Malham. All roads lead to Malham. It's all happening in Malham. It's a never-ending party in Malham. Like Sinatra said: 'If you can make it there, you can make it back as well'.'

I couldn't tell whether he was speaking with civic pride or sarcasm, but I gave him the benefit of the doubt, then thanked him and climbed on.

I did not see much of Burnley. Not much you *can* see from the bus station. A cocktail lounge bar called Carpe Diem – 'seize the day' – a bus service to somewhere called Bleak House, and a bus tour called The Witch Way, presumably named after Pendle Hill, which loomed oppressively on the horizon. It seemed strange that I had to cross the Yorkshire border into Lancashire, just to reach another part of Yorkshire. But the other route was longer, involving three trains, two buses and a whole lot of standing around waiting for connections, some of which seldom connected. This route from Halifax to Burnley by train, then Burnley to Malham by bus, was quicker and hassle-free.

Although I had never been to Burnley, it seemed somehow familiar, with the town much like my own. All I could see was a mere cover version of my everyday surroundings in Halifax. The traffic, the townies, the bustle and hustle, the hustle and hassle, almost-identical streets and highways, shopping precincts, offices, factories.

While still in the town centre, a mother and daughter climbed on the bus arguing, possibly since they left the house, continuing their domestic disagreements on the bus. Neither would back down, both valiantly attempting to publicly embarrass the other into silence, though neither showing signs of shame or humiliation. They had both made their minds up. Their dirty laundry was going to get a thorough scrubbing in public and too bad if the smell makes everyone gip.

The bus moved on through a succession of other built-up areas, like Nelson and Colne which, at first glance, seemed little different from Burnley, but as the bus scuttled on, stopping at traffic lights, giving way, pulling out, negotiating the assault course of the crowded roads, the busy towns and their suburbs began to dwindle away, and small greens on grass verges became gigantic greens on village verges, together with the stalking fear, creeping into my thoughts, my bones, my very soul. For this is the fear that comes with going somewhere you've never been, on your own, into the wilderness, where anything could happen, you could disappear, never be seen again.

We arrived at Barnoldswick, which is a record breaker for two reasons. Firstly, it's the largest town in Britain not to be served by any A-roads. And secondly, Barnoldswick is one of the longest place names in the UK – without repeating any letters. The others are Buckfastleigh in Devon and two places called Buslingthorpe, one in Leeds and the other in Lincolnshire. Who sets themselves the task of working out these things? And, more to the point, why? It's hardly something worthwhile to include on your CV. Hobbies? Interests? Counting the letters in place names, paying particular attention to those words in which the letters are not repeated.

As the bus stopped at Barnoldswick, a group of young women climbed on, avidly discussing why some character from Eastenders wants to get married to someone else, and why she would be much better off without him, while sounding genuinely shocked and horrified in the process. I found their conversation truly amazing. I've watched *Doctor Who*, and I've enjoyed it, but I don't gossip with friends saying 'Those pesky Cybermen! Invading the Earth and trying to vaporize the Doctor. Honestly! The barefaced cheek of it! Who do they think they are? The Daleks?'

The bus stopped at Malham. The buildings are constructed from the sort of grey stone that you only get in out-of-the-way places. And despite the number of visitors, there are no crowds – just small groups of hikers and day-trippers, and very little sound, as if the visitors want to maintain the peace and quiet, like students in a library. I clambered off the bus, and rushed to the little stone bridge, peered into the Aire. It was already flowing. But flowing from where? Where did it start? I need to find the source.

So my first stop was at the Information Centre, and my first question was: 'Where is the source of the River Aire?'

'It's just there,' said the assistant helpfully, if a little confusingly, pointing through the window, as if I had missed the river gushing through the village.

'Does it start here?' I asked

Blank look and silence.

'Where is the source of the Aire? Where does it start?'

'It flows through Malham.'

'Yes. I know it flows *through* Malham. I want to know where it flows *from*.'

Blank look and silence.

'I mean, where does it start?'

More blank looks.

For goodness sake, I thought. It's not *Mastermind* or *The Krypton Factor*. It's a simple question really.

'I must have made a mistake. I'm sorry. I thought this was an information centre.'

'It is an information centre,' said one of the women, clear agitation in her voice.

'Great! Well, see if you can wrap your brain around this simple enough concept. Where - does - the - river - Aire - flow - from? Where - does - it - start?'

They look at each other.

'It flows *through* the village of Malham, which *you* are *currently* in.'

You may think I'm making this up to inject a little humour into the narrative. But, honestly, this conversation *really* happened – with the exception of the 'brain-wrapping' bit, which I added for good measure.

'We don't live around here,' she said apologetically.

That's helpful. Surely one of the points in the job description would have been 'must have considerable knowledge of the local area' not to mention 'a firm grasp of the English language.'

Eventually, I left the centre with a clutch of leaflets, resigned to ploughing through all the uninspired factual guff and finding the location of the source myself.

One of the leaflets read: 'Malham is a village and civil parish in the Craven District of North Yorkshire.'

No. I knew that already.

'Malham Tarn is a glacial lake. It is 377 metres above sea level, making it the highest lake in England.'

Well, I *didn't* know that. But then I didn't honestly care. What did they think I was? A tourist?

Limestone – no. Waterfall – no.

Gordale Scar. Janet's Foss. The Source.

A-ha!

'The primary outflow is a small stream at the southern end of Malham Tarn. The outflow stream goes underground after approximately 500 metres before emerging downstream of Malham Cove as a source of the River Aire.'

Yuppee-Da!

So I asked a local man how to reach the tarn and learned it was a further two miles up the valley. I should head for Malham Cove, then climb the stone steps, walk through Gordale Scar, and along to the Tarn. Besides, a trip to Malham wouldn't be complete without the Cove, the Scar and the Tarn. So I had a brisk walk up the country road, through a gate, and then followed the path through fields, amid an assortment of other hikers dressed in bright coloured cagoules, pants and rucksacks, moving like a swarm of multi-coloured Buddhists on a pilgrimage to the Cove, which towers over the valley. Even though it is a massive monument, you cannot see it in its entirety at any point on the path, shrouded as it is in trees, as if Mother Nature herself has planted them there to stop people making do with seeing it at a distance, as if saying 'there is a magnificent natural beauty beyond these trees, but if you want to see it all, you must make an extra effort.' I hate it when uninspired travel writers use clichéd terms like 'breathtaking' and 'awe-inspiring' to describe some natural monument or landmark. But now I'm going to be a hypocrite and commit the same crime, because I honestly can't think of better words to describe the Cove. It is definitely breathtaking and awe-inspiring.

Halfway along the path we pass a herd of cows munching quietly on the grass, ignoring the thru-hikers, and I reached a man in a Landrover, parked by the path, with leaflets from the National Trust, offering people membership. I can't afford to sign up, but I pop a pound in the collection tin and head off for the next gate, as the National Trust guy says to a couple who sign-up with them: 'Oh no, here they come. They always come and bother me.' I turn to see the cows approaching his vehicle. First, one of them head-butts the National Trust sign and knocks it over. So the man sighs and picks it up, only for another one to head-butt it again. This happens two or three times. As some of them distract him, a few others sneak their way to the rear of the vehicle and peer through the windows, looking tough and threatening, like bovine bouncers. As the man goes to shoo them away, another cow head-butts the sign and it crashes down again.

At the next gate, there was a sign, which read: 'This way to the free *Aren't Birds Brilliant?* Viewpoint'. Two men and a woman, members of the RSPB, have two cameras, each with viewfinders pointing up at a specific ledge on the Cove, and we visitors wait in turn to peer through the viewfinder. There is no charge for this service and, although they are touting membership forms, it still comes as something of a shock.

Free? Free of charge? Is this a joke?

'Are you sure,' said a foreign visitor. 'You want nothing?'

'Nothing, madam, really,' smiled one of the members.

This doesn't seem to sink in.

'I can't afford much. But I can give you a little.'

He politely turned down the offer, and although there was a donation tin nearby, he did not draw attention to it.

A peregrine falcon, one of the men told me, is the fastest living creature on Earth. When it swoops down on prey it has been clocked at a speed of 280 miles per hour. As we peered through the viewfinder, he tells us we are viewing a juvenile peregrine falcon. It sits at the edge of the ledge. Are there many of them at the Cove, I ask. No, says the man. Only one pair exists here. And the birds have several 'pantries' or 'larders' on the cove, in the guise of small caves, where they store all their food. The one I can see on the ledge is in one such pantry and, as I watch, it scuttles back inside for a spot of nosh.

Further on, over some slippery rocks and I'm at the foot of the Cove, which is truly breathtaking and awe-inspiring. (Oops! I've done it again!) This amazing natural wonder gives the impression that some mischievous cosmic deity has nicked a coastal cliff and stuck it in the middle of inland Yorkshire just for a giggle. Not that it looks out of place. It is formed from limestone which is evident in the boulders and farm walls of the area, and so it sort of blends in with the surroundings. The precarious stumble along the banks of the Aire has been well worth it. The Cove is the haunt of various teams of rock climbers, some in pairs, other groups of more, with their irons stuck in the rocks above. With their ropes and harnesses strapped tightly around them, they begin to scale the heights. There are a set of steps to the left of the Cove, gouged out of the rock, and so begins the climb up. The famous limestone pavement at the top is like a patchwork of giant, grey stepping stones, with cracks in-between.

Another short walk and I end up in Gordale Scar. I've seen the gorge, (or dry valley, as it's known) in countless TV documentaries, and on calendars and postcards and in travel books, but no matter how great the graphics and Technicolor are, no matter how convenient it is to see photographs of it in a magazine or book, there really is no substitute for being there. Not only is it amazing to behold, but also to walk through it, entirely alone, is an experience in itself. It is a dry day, not too sunny and warm, but not cold and unwelcoming either. I am constantly having to watch my step, stumbling over these natural rocks which line the valley from tip to end, which could twist or break an ankle with one small slip.

I climb over a stile and there's a notice-board, which reads: 'If the cows become agitated by your dog and chase or crowd around you, let the dog off the lead – don't risk getting hurt by protecting it. The cows should follow the dog which will be able to outrun them, leaving you to continue along the path.'

I nod in agreement. There's a time for selfless heroism – but this isn't it. Besides, this is your chance of getting your own back on the mangy mutt for refusing to urinate during your long walk in the park, then returning home to pee on the begonias.

As I make my way through the gorge, this lonely natural pass, peering at steep sides of the cliffs overhead, I realise that this valley (or its twin) has been featured in many a horror film, with me doubling as the poor schmuck, dead as a dodo, long before the hero turns up to save the day.

Indeed, I am convinced that the hills have eyes and are alive (but not with the sound of music) and I can't quite shake the sensation that someone is watching me from above, but a quick darting look reveals nothing.

In his account of his search for Dr Livingstone, Henry Morton Stanley wrote: 'I may say I am alone in a wild country'. Bearing in mind that he *was* alone in a wild country, it seemed a pointless comment for the celebrated journalist, who was widely revered for his perceptive writing. But here *I* am, certainly alone in a wild part of the *county*. Admittedly, it does not make fascinating reading but, by God, it's true! I trudge through countless fields, which the rain has turned into marshland, until I reach Malham Tarn.

This is where the author Charles Kingsley (brother of explorer Mary Kingsley) visited when he got the inspiration for his novel *The Water Babies*. I won't pretend I've read it, or have any intention of doing so, just for the purpose of displaying how well read I am, (which I'm not) so I'll just leave it hanging in the air in a mysterious and mystical way, as I make my way to the edge of the tarn.

It is so quiet here. Truly rural. Not even passenger jets are racing overhead as if the airport authorities have agreed to keep this part of the world free of all noise, including the overhead drone of those poor souls who believe they have to fling themselves to foreign shores to escape the relentless jabber of civilised commotion.

As I said before, Malham Tarn is the highest lake in Britain, 377 metres above sea level. It is also a glacial lake. I'm not sure what this means, but I'll check it out. It's also Britain's highest 'marl' lake (don't ask) and is one of only eight upland alkaline lakes in the whole of Europe, having a pH of between 8.0 and 8.6. (Huh?) The catchment area of the lake is 600 hectares and the lake's basin was damned by something called a moraine, at the end of the last glacial period approx 10,000 years ago... you've probably guessed that I'm nicking all this from a tourist leaflet. But the information offered uses unfamiliar academic words, without any sort of explanation as to what they mean. So I have little to write about the tarn. It's a big lake, surrounded by countryside in the middle of nowhere. It is also a nice lake, but it's no nicer or any different to any of the other lakes or tarns or reservoirs that I have seen in my time.

In my view, a writer should be just that. Someone who writes from first-hand experience, or inspiration, or both. Been there, done that, soiled the T-shirt. In theory, I could have written this book without ever leaving home, just hooked myself up to the internet, typed all the destinations along the River Aire into a search engine, nicked loads of information from the world wide web, thrown in a few one-liners for good measure and promoted myself as a world weary traveller; so weary that I couldn't even be bothered to pull on my walking boots. But in my view, a writer needs to go places. Experience life first-hand, then report back to the readers. And perhaps – like Amundsen – even suffer a little, so his or her readers don't have to. I really *did* go to these places, armed only with a pen, a notebook, an enquiring mind, and a willingness to get wet and muddy for the purposes of literary entertainment, and vowed never to use the library or internet for research. And, as I scribble away, I really *am* standing on the edge of Malham Tarn. I just have nothing else to say about it.

I sat on the grass by the tarn and, rather rashly, munched through my entire stock of Snickers. I got the idea of packing Snickers (which are really just *Marathons* to British readers) from Bill Bryson's book *A Walk in the Woods*, and Mr Bryson used to live up here in Malhamdale, and no doubt visited this very tarn, so I tried to draw some inspiration from his past presence as I sat there scribbling away. With all the food supplies gone, and still hungry, I see an ice-cream van parked near the tarn. Strange. I didn't see it before. Could it have been a mirage? Designed to fool the famished traveller, like the hot-dog-stand in the desert that appears to Laurel and Hardy in the film *Beau Chumps*? But as I stumble forward, it remains visible, so I grab a choc-ice and head back along the road past a sign which reads: 'Malham 2 miles.'

'I wouldn't go that way, luv,' the ice-cream woman calls out to me. 'All the tourists go that way. They think the two miles is nothing, but it's two miles of hills and dales. And two miles can seem like six on a rollercoaster road like that.'

So I thank her and plump for the road less travelled, which could have been entirely un-travelled, as there seems to be no-one except sheep for miles around and the road, as promised, turns out to be a combination of straight-alongs and down-hills, all the way back to Malham.

'Hello, sheep!' I greet them. 'What a great place to live!'

My greeting is met with nothing but white spots of bleating wool, munching grass and vacant stares with dead, glassy eyes.

But what sort of welcome was I expecting? A toe-tapping, disco-dancing, knees-up-mother-brown extravaganza, spectacularly choreographed by the Busby Berkeley of animal husbandry? This is the sort of thing a struggling writer thinks about, stood in the middle of nowhere, in some remote and bleak landscape, cut off from other people, and desperately trying to dream-up a book, to impress readers with their literary ability and wit.

Is it working?

I would love to know what farm animals think about. Sheep, cattle, pigs, chickens, even horses. What do they *think* about? They *can* certainly, but they don't think in words, only concepts. What would *we* think about if we were forcibly located to the countryside? In the event of war, with towns and cities engulfed in noxious and choking fumes, the survivors would be herded out into the country. And what would we do? Like being marooned on an island, would society cease to speak?

Would we continue to think in words – or would our thoughts be limited to concepts and situations, day and night, brightness and darkness, light and colour? There would no longer be a comparison between noisy and quiet, stress and serene. It would just be still and un-rushed. Watches and clocks would run down and cease to function, and so eventually time would mean nothing. Would we all go silently potty, faced with the remoteness of it all? Out here, it's surely tranquil and serene, but no one can hear you scream.

The idea of living in the wilderness – any wilderness – has a tendency to scare people, and so it has done for centuries. But the open countryside really *is* the safest place to be, compared to crowded towns and cities. How much crime and violence is there out here in the country? And how many really wild animals could do you serious harm in rural Britain? The fear of the open country is largely irrational. But what would it be like to sleep out here?

Robert Louis Stevenson mused on the subject: 'Night is a dead monotonous period under a roof; but in the open world it passes lightly, with its stars and dews and perfumes, and the hours are marked by changes in the face of Nature. What seems a kind of temporal death to people choked between walls and curtains, is only a light and living slumber to the man who sleeps afield. All night long he can hear Nature breathing deeply and freely... The outer world, from which we cower in our houses, seemed after all a gentle habitable place.'

I love the countryside. But I speak as a townie. I love to go to the country, but only as a blessed relief of being in town. And I love walking in the countryside as long as I know I can return to the hustle and bustle alongside my fellow sapien, whenever I feel like it. If we had to live in the wilds indefinitely what would we do all day? Well, probably what livestock do. Eat, Drink, Sleep, Crap, and stare at visitors through our vacant, glassy eyes. As it happens, we humans are more intelligent than mere livestock. We are civilised and highly evolved, so we eat, drink, sleep, crap and stare at our televisions with vacant, glassy eyes, then work like mad to pay for the privilege. Still. It beats chewing the cud, pulling your pud, and stood in the mud.

Doesn't it?

I glance down at my ragged dog-eared notebook, with hastily scribbled notes of my thoughts, witticisms, musings, and wonder - not for the first time - why I opted to write a travelogue instead of a guidebook. Providing entertainment for the armchair traveller is infinitely more difficult than providing information for the actual traveller. Research for a guidebook would simply involve taking a few photos, raiding the tourist information centres of all their leaflets and maps, or some learned website as demonstrated above, (failing that, plagiarising *Rough Guides* and *Lonely Planets*), pretending I've been to places, stood by tarns, and read classic novels by authors like Charles Kingsley, then returning home to re-hash it on my computer, leaving the design and imagination and marketing and binding and advertising and selling to the publisher, while I got on with the next one.

But a travelogue is the sort of soul-searching document that takes ages to do. And then there's the question: which soul-searches should I include, and which should be discarded at all costs? Should I have discarded this whole paragraph, for example? If Carlsberg wrote travelogues, they would be much better than this one. Well, probably.

It's OK speaking this aloud, as I know there is no one but me and the mutton for miles around.

Just then, a man and woman pop their heads over a nearby wall. They have no doubt been picnicking, and they peer across at me wondering why I am talking to a sheep. I feel immediately embarrassed and wonder how I can get out of this one - but I have an idea. Luckily, they can only see me sideways, from my right, so I quickly plunge my left hand into my coat pocket, make a grab for my mobile phone and clamp it to my ear, and then swing round conspicuously to face them head-on.

"Hello," I say loudly into my phone, so the onlookers can hear. "Are you still there, Sheep? Are you OK? Good. I say, you don't mind me calling you Sheep, do you? It is a silly nickname, but I like it. Ha-ha-ha! There's a couple over here, who probably think I've been talking to a sheep, since I am out here, otherwise alone, and surrounded by sheep. Ha-ha-ha! They must think I'm mad. Whereas, they now realise their folly. Because I am talking to you, my friend, whose nickname is actually 'Sheep', for reasons hardly worth exploring for the benefit of this short rural discourse. Ha-ha-ha! OK, then. See you later. Bye."

The couple are still looking at me strangely, so I look down at my left hand, which is holding not a phone, but a forgotten Snickers bar. I take a deep breath, and decide to press ahead sharpish.

Chapter Three

Back at Malham, I enter the Barn Shop Café. I am so tired I can only manage to order a pot of tea and sit down. My boots are caked with mud, but I can't be bothered to remove them. That's OK. This must be the only café in the world with a sign outside reading 'Muddy Boots Welcome'. I think the proprietors would prefer muddy boots to smelly socks. At least mud can be scrubbed away, while smells can linger forever and become eternal nasal nightmares.

There is much at Malham to intrigue the visitor – but the intrigue is not man-made. It is natural intrigue. How was this beautiful part of the world created? And who or what created it? Whether you believe in a God – or simply Mother Nature – who-dun-it doesn't really matter, because whoever done it, done it real well. However, despite this natural intrigue, carved out of limestone and water and grass, there are, occasionally, other kinds of intrigue.

In May 2006, an electrician was called to Malham Parish Hall to do a check-up so they could attain a safety certificate. But what he found amazed everyone. Hidden in a 13-amp wall socket, he found an electronic transmitter – a bugging device – used by the security services for covert operations, which has a range of several hundred metres. The caretaker and treasurer of the hall, Alan Boatwright said: 'I was absolutely gobsmacked. I have showed it to various people and everyone has been falling about laughing. It has been the talk of the Dale. This is Malham – population 120 – and, despite being a tourist village, nothing goes on here. This really has made everyone's day. Maybe the covert listener is a fan of the Women's Institute singing *Jerusalem*, or he might have been listening to the whist drive.' The bug was handed to North Yorkshire Police for analysis, but no further news of it has come to light.

Many explorers were struck with melancholy on their expeditions. Henry Morton Stanley wrote: 'Now that I am faced with inhospitable Africa there is something, it seems to me, which grinds out all hope of return.'

Mary Kingsley shared the sentiment. In her book *Travels in West Africa*, she writes: 'I do not recommend the African forest life to anyone. Unless you are interested in it and fall under its charm, it is the most awful life in death imaginable. It is like being shut up in a library whose books you cannot read, all the while tormented, terrified and bored. And if you do fall under its spell, it takes all the colour out of other kinds of living.'

When Bonpland and Humboldt arrived in the Llanos, the latter wrote: 'Everything here makes one think of the world in its primeval state. The fatigue of travelling beneath a burning sky, the eternal thirst one feels… the view of a horizon which seems forever in retreat – all these causes combine to make the Llanos melancholy and depressing.'

Oh, quit complaining. Some people, all they do is complain. What did they all expect? A merry jaunt in the wilds of Yorkshire? Well, that's what I expected. And wasn't disappointed. So I *do* recommend Malham to anyone and everyone, and a trip to the village will inject colour and zest into everywhere else you go. If you fall under its spell, if you stay here too long, you may not want to leave. Despite being known as a 'tourist village' Malham has not been spoilt – not yet anyway – with scores of shops selling crap holiday gear, Kiss-Me-Quick hats and lots of sticky, fluffy and gooey foods which shops like this tend to offer. Folk come here to get away from all that guff and they will not be disappointed.

After my tea, I set off again, away from Malham. Just out of the village, I saw a farm over to my right, populated by strange looking creatures, which I could not identify at such a distance. They were either miniature camels, deformed giraffes, genetically modified sheep (modified, for what reason I don't know) or llamas. Eventually, I decided on the latter.

Why do British farmers breed llamas? Is it so they can form a society called *Farmers who breed Llamas*, and show off at agricultural conventions? And, if so, why do things by halves? Why not go the whole poetic hog and call themselves *Farmers are Charmers who breed Llamas in Pyjamas*. Though whether it is the farmers or the llamas that wear the pyjamas, doesn't seem to matter. There had to be a more practical reason. As I trudged down the valley, across a small, seemingly insubstantial stream (the mighty River Aire, as it turned out) the farmer came into the field to do whatever farmers do. I leaned over the wall and called out to him.

'Why llamas?'

'Why not?'

I walked straight through the village of Hanlith and only realised it when I had reached the other side. I can't tell you much about it but, if you ever find yourself here, in desperate need of fresh free-range eggs, then Rookery Cottage is probably your best bet.

My first dilemma. The path wandered left, while the river turned right. I could either follow the flow of the river and venture into private land, maybe walk for a couple of miles, get threatened with a shotgun and have to turn back and re-trace my steps. So I kept with the footpath. Much of the river was on private land. And while the new Rights of Way had made great progress for hikers, there were still huge tracts of farmland flanking the Aire, which offered no access to the public at all. People don't actually own land. Do they? Well, they don't. Who was it who first thought 'I own this land, and therefore I can sell it'?

I had been looking forward to visiting Bell Busk, a small hamlet along the Aire, not least to explore the reason behind the curious name. Was it the haunt of a busker who could play nothing but a bell? Apparently, there was a guesthouse, converted from an old train station. But it wasn't exactly on the Aire, but two miles down a lane, so I made an executive decision and skipped it, because I wanted to stick with the river and reach Gargrave before it got dark. Just past the turn-off, I climbed up a steep hill with wide sweeping views. A perfect place for pacifists to sit and watch thousands of soldiers slaughter each other, with the working classes duped into power struggles of the ruling classes, as usual, with land or pride as the prize, a battle fuelled by vested interests, thinly disguised as moral principles.

I approached a field full of cows and stopped dead. One of them had horns. Was it a bull? Or a cow with horns? I didn't know if cows could have horns, without being bulls. I scoured the field for evidence of a homicidal bull, but there was a distinct lack of warning signs and gored hikers. There was a stile, which suggested this was a public right of way, so I decided to be a macho man and push on ahead. As I did so, the bull – or horned cow – looked up, then straight at me. I hesitated.

In his book *The Art of Travel* (1872), Francis Galton writes about his various encounters not with bulls, but mules: 'Mules require men who know their habits; they are powerful beasts, and can only be mastered with skill... They have odd secret ways, strange fancies and lurking vice.'

Although this was a bull, I had no reason to suspect it did not possess its own odd secret ways, lurking vice (whatever that is) and strange fancies (I didn't even want to ponder what this meant). Would a bull be more amenable to the weary traveller, than a mule? I did not want to risk it, and so reversed over the stile. Although there is a difference between a bull and a mule it would not be a distinction I would feel compelled to make, if I reached halfway through the field and it charged me, for a bull could be ferocious in its own way – perhaps more so than a mule. It was certainly no chicken, and too bulky – in all the wrong places – to be a Spring chicken. But regardless of its intentions, I plumped for plodding the perimeter, deciding that detours were grossly underrated.

Within the first hour, I passed two huge trees, keeled over near the river, broken apart by something obviously powerful, though I could not tell whether the culprit was heavy winds, lightening, or giant squirrels, so I kept a sharp lookout.

The village of Airton was larger than Hanlith, probably the size of Malham, give or take. The road ran past some smart stone houses, flanked on the other side by a spacious village green. I looked at the village notice board and someone called Charlotte Turner was raising money so she could be a contender in something called the Tall Ships Race. I hope she won.

When I lost the river, I followed the road. Then I thought I saw the river, so I left the road and found, instead, a small stream. Instead of retracing my steps, I took what I thought was a short cut, which would probably lead me back to the road, and would in turn lead me back to the river. It did not. So now I was not only river-less but road-less. I was climbing a hill, away from a river. Away from anything, in fact, other than grass. Leave roads to their own devices and they are sensible. Particularly rural roads, which follow generally acceptable rules of behaviour. It's only when planners start mucking about with them, re-directing them, making them into underpasses, flyovers and – when they feel peckish – spaghetti junctions, that the problems really begin.

Rivers, on the other hand, spend a lot of time showing off by trying to escape the weary traveller. First they will look amiable and approachable and then, without warning, they veer off erratically and at great speed like Formula One, scarpering into the distance through private land. It seemed determined to escape from me. But I realised what the Aire was doing. It was testing me, to see if I could stand the pace, to see if I had the stamina to keep up with it, to see if I was a committed river walker, not some aimless and half-hearted rambler. The Aire only wanted serious hikers – not timewasters. So I was stood in the field, miles from anywhere and far from everywhere, with somewhere thinly disguised as nowhere – my only companion.

At this point, I considered performing my 'jump-up-and-down-on-the-map-I-can't-believe-I-paid-good-money-for-this-crap-those-thieving-blighters' routine, but decided against it, as it would not help my cause one iota. So I plumped for the less athletic, but equally unhelpful, sit-down-roll-a-fag-and-feel-sorry-for-myself routine, which worked a treat. At this point, I wondered if I was really cut out for this exploring lark.

That celebrated explorer of the Middle East, Freya Stark, listed the ten qualities which she said were required by the traveller, and I measured myself against them:

I)   A temper as serene at the end of the day as at the beginning.

II)   The capacity to accept other people's standards.

III)   Rapid judgement of character.

IV)   A love of nature including human nature.

V)   The capacity to disassociate oneself from bodily sensations.

VI)   A knowledge of local history and language.

VII)   A leisurely and uncensorious mind.

VIII) A tolerable constitution.

IX)   The ability to eat and sleep at any moment.

X)   A ready quickness in repartee.

All of the above made sense to me, except the last. I thought it highly unlikely I would get ambushed by a tribe of comedy cannibals, firing a volley of rubber arrows, with survival entirely dependent on my ability to reel off a stock of witty one-liners and clever ripostes. But what do I know? Freya Stark was a seasoned explorer. I am not.

But what was the problem anyway? I wasn't stuck in the middle of a punch-up between a lion and tiger. I wasn't being chased over the Antarctic by a giant walrus, with my screams and cries echoing across the glaciers. And I hadn't come down with malaria or scurvy. I was stuck in a field in the Yorkshire Dales on a warm and sunny day. There were certainly much worse places to be, so I decided it was time to pull myself together.

To relax, I started to unfasten my laces, to remove the boots and acquaint my feet with the soft grass and fresh air for a change, but remembered a quote from Mary Kingsley who – would you believe – took her carpet slippers into the jungle with her! She wrote: 'It never does in this country to leave off boots altogether at any time and risk getting bitten by mosquitoes on the feet when you are on the march. The rub of your boot on the bite always produces a sore, and a sore when it comes in the gorilla country comes to stay.'

As I pulled on my boots, I glanced up to see a rather healthy-looking man with white hair, accompanied by a small black & white dog, striding through the field. So I strode towards them, introduced myself and asked if he knew the direction to Gargrave.

'I live there,' he said. 'Yorkshire Dales! Best countryside in the world. Know this area like the back of my front. I trudge through it every day. You're welcome to tag along.'

His name was Ron and he had opted for early retirement from his office job, after which he and his wife had sold the house and bought a narrowboat. They now spent the year travelling up and down Britain's canal network, currently moored on the canal at Gargrave. The boat had a name, which I forget now, something like Linzo Zenzo, which sounds like one of the Marx Brothers, and they liked it, and so didn't change it. However, a year later, Ron and his missus discovered that the name was Swahili for 'Bugger Off'. They still kept the name, though, thinking it was a good icebreaker; a good conversation point.

Ron was armed with an Ordnance Survey map, the best kind by far, and the most accurate of all maps, which includes all sorts of details that other maps don't, including the exact location of all public rights of way.

Didn't help him though. We walked in circles for the best part of an hour, until Ron suddenly stopped.

'That's funny,' he said, looking directly ahead. A caravan was parked at the edge of the next field under some trees. 'That wasn't there when I walked up here, on this oh-so-glorious morn. And it don't do-look like it did just arrived, do it?'

'No,' I agreed, trying to make sense of this apparent linguistic logic. 'It did do-it not.'

The caravan looked like it pre-dated the Ark, and had probably been here since the Flintstones got evicted. So we set off along a track, over a fence, through a field, over another fence (which did a cracking impression of the first fence) and onto a country track, which looked strangely familiar, before Ron stopped so abruptly that I nearly bumped into him.

'That's funny' he said.

If this was funny to Ron, I didn't admire his sense of humour. It was clear we were never going to agree on the principles of good comedy.

'That tree looks familiar. And there's another old caravan.'

We stopped a couple of cyclists, who looked as if they were clearly intent on running us down if we didn't leave them alone. But they helped us, and eventually, we bumbled over a bridge and Gargrave hit us full on. We stopped at a pub. He offered me a pint but I had stopped drinking by then, so I got a pint of icy cool orange. I thanked Ron and bade farewell, then went for a brief stroll through the village.

Everything in Gargrave seems to be housed in a pretty cottage, including the Dalesman Café and Tea Rooms, and even the local Indian restaurant and takeaway: Bollywood

Cottage. I didn't see much else. There was a sign reading: 'Roman Gargrave', and I found the river again as it gushed busily under a grand stone-arched bridge. I wanted to stay longer, but set off again, clambering over a wall, trying to keep track of the Aire, which I had just found after a long absence. I scuttled through some trees, and nearly ran into a man dressed in a smart blue uniform and peaked cap.

'It's private property,' he said, pointing to a sign, which had nothing on it.

'It doesn't say so.'

'Ah, no. They're being replaced, see. Nice new posh, laminated glossy ones.'

'Why didn't they keep the old signs, until the new ones had arrived?'

'......'

'That would make more sense.'

'......'

'More sense, so that you would never be without signs, and people like me wouldn't keep trespassing, and people like you wouldn't have to keep telling people like me to get off private property. Wouldn't that be better?'

'That's not my department, see. Not my problem."

'Whose problem is it?'

'Not mine.'

So I return to the road, passing a company called Johnson and Johnson Wound Management, and wonder if this is an accident blackspot. Here, the river runs through private farmland. With a choice between road and canal, I opt for the latter, and can follow the towpath while keeping a weather eye on the Aire, tracking it from afar, as it continues to snake back and forth like a wily python.

One of the great things about the Yorkshire Dales is that five minutes in bus or car, leaving behind the population centres, and you can suddenly and overwhelmingly be in total rurality. Fifteen minutes out of Gargrave – even on foot – and you've got a 360-degree scope of rural country: fields, forests, farms, hills, and the occasional inn, which continues for the seven miles to Skipton.

I was getting a bit peckish and regretted wolfing down the chocolate bars at Malham Tarn in a severe attack of personal greed. And that was my second lesson about expeditions. Always pack enough grub. More than you need, just in case.

Dr Livingstone once found himself short of food supplies. He wrote: 'We were surprised next day by our black cook from Sierra Leone bearing in a second course. 'What have you got there?' was asked in wonder. 'A tart, sir.' 'A tart! Of what is it made?' 'Of cabbage, sir.' As we had no sugar, and could not 'make believe' as in the days of boyhood, we did not enjoy the feast that Tom's genius had prepared.'

And Livingstone wasn't the only one whose tummy started to rumble in the jungle. Henry Morton Stanley and his mob, who went searching for Livingstone, also found themselves short of rations. Stanley wrote: 'Our store of sugar had run out… our coffee was finished at Vinya-Njara, and at Inkisi Falls our tea, alas! alas! Came to an end.'

They were forced to take what they could find, including '…three fried bananas, twenty roasted nuts, a cup of muddy water. First we rinsed in clear brook water from the ravines some choice cassava and manioc tops, and these were placed in the water to be bruised, (and so we) rejoiced our stomachs and souls with the savoury mess.'

I peered at the canal. Although the water in the Aire was clear, the stagnant canal was all muck and murk. I didn't want to be rinsing or bruising any of my ingredients in there.

Besides, mist and murk can contain all sorts of nasties, with long, scientific-sounding, scary names like Leptospirosis – of which Weil's Disease is a severe form, which comes from the bacterium of rats, mice, cattle, dogs and pigs, which can enter through skin abrasion, or lining of the mouth, nose, throat, or eyes. Bilharzia – also known with the tongue-twister name of schistosmiasis – is caused by a parasitic flatworm, which lives in slow-moving freshwater streams and – no doubt – non-moving canals. Amoebic Dysentry is contracted by drinking water contaminated by infected sewage. Giardiasis is caused by a parasite, resident in water contaminated with infected urine or faeces. And finally, something sinister called Hookworms, can enter the human body in drinking water or directly through the skin.

What I wanted, instead, was a proper rejoicing of stomach and soul, without any symptoms such as meningitis, haemorrhaging, kidney failure, abdominal cramps or heart damage. All this just because I was a little peckish.

So I decided to put my hunger on hold, then pig-out in Skipton.

Chapter Four

The name Skipton comes from the words 'sheep' and 'ton'. A ton of sheep? This was slightly disappointing. I was hoping it had something to do with either a strange custom of skipping or an incredibly perceptive bush kangaroo.

You can tell a well-heeled town, with customers from the country set, by a simple walk down the high street. There is always a branch of Ponden Mill (though what they sell, I've never discovered), and Skipton was no exception.

I was now quite hungry, but faced with overpriced restaurants, which looked great – and underpriced cafes, which didn't – I had a sarny and a cuppa in Subway. Being a socialist, I like to slag off big companies wherever and whenever, but it was nice. Nice food, nice atmosphere, nice staff. After dinner (or 'lunch' if you went to grammar school, or 'liquid lunch' if you're a white-collar alcoholic) I bought lots of pop from a shop, and decide to sit on the canal wall and take it easy for a while, guzzling the cans of pop one after the other.

On his quest for Livingstone, Stanley came down with malaria and so drugged himself with quinine. His diary entry reads: 'I am in such a state tonight that I can neither lie down or sit quietly in one position long. I am nervous and my head is very strange. I have the most fearful dreams every night and am afraid to shut my eyes, lest I shall see the horrid things that haunt me. I will go walk, walk, walk in the forest to get rid of them.'

I knew what he meant. I felt much the same after three cans of *Irn Bru*.

As I had covered some real distance already and as the darkness was creeping up, it was time to call it a day and head home, which always gave me a sad feeling. The expedition was far from finished. In fact, it had barely begun. I've always felt that a journey should be a one-off thing. You set off from home, do the whole thing, and only return when completed. I bet Captain Scott or Captain Cook never did one day of travelling, then had to go home, work another week for crap money, and then return to do another weekend, spending valuable hours in-between, travelling to-and-from the destination on public transport. Marco Polo or Stanley and Livingstone wouldn't be seen dead stood on a freezing train platform, south-east from the back of beyond, bang-slap in middling nowhere, waiting in vain for bus or train, then told there'll be a delay, for no apparent reason. I began to feel a bit envious. But then that's life, and you've got to play it the best you can with whatever you've got. So I call it a day, get the train home, and the next weekend, I am back on a train travelling from Bradford Forster Square, heading for Skipton.

The trains from this station seem infinitely more pleasant than the trains from Bradford Interchange, or anywhere else for that matter. Not the scenery, for there was little different from anywhere else, similar terraced houses, identical roads, forgettable suburbs. There were some places we passed through and I tried to avert my eyes from them, as many were urban trading posts – Shipley, Saltaire, Crossflatts, Bingley, Keighley – which I was destined to pass through on this journey and I didn't want to catch sight of them before I arrived, as it could spoil any surprises that my expedition yet had in store for me. The train journey itself was the pleasing part. The going was smooth, the suspension incredible, as the train glided like Luke Skywalker's hovercar. The only sound was the heaven's breath air-conditioning, with only the occasional bump on the track as we ran over a hoodie.

It was such smooth and silent running that we pulled so gracefully into Skipton train station, that I wouldn't have realised it, were it not for the immensely irritating voice on the intercom.

'Welcome to the train to Skipton. This is the train to Skipton. The next station is Skipton. In fact, this station is Skipton. You're at Skipton now. This train terminates here. Here being Skipton. When we arrive at Skipton – which we already have – please ensure that you leave the train. Please vacate the carriage as soon as possible… Like now, for example.'

I clambered off, and scribbled something in my notebook. I had decided I would have to write this book on the road. I could not rely on memory alone. I needed a written record of the journey to be completed as soon as I thought of something original or pithy or, occasionally, intelligent.

Many explorers kept a diary on their expeditions. On his travels in Arabia, explorer Charles Montagu Doughty was curious about everything he encountered, recording it all at length in his notebooks, which then formed part of his highly acclaimed book *Travels in Arabia Deserta* (1888). It caused him trouble at times. Some people considered him to be a spy, while others thought he was attempting to gain some kind of power over them, by committing them in symbolic form to paper.

I had similar trouble alighting the train, when a woman gave me a nervous glance as I scribbled away. She peered across at me, eyes narrowing, brows furrowing, paranoia paying a visit. Her eyes seemed to ask: '*Who* are you? *What* are you? A British Rail official? A private detective? He's my best friend's boyfriend. I didn't touch him. I wouldn't do really. I was just being friendly. I'm not kinky. And the feather was just a joke. Please don't tell anyone. I won't do it again.'

'Relax,' my eyes say. 'I'm writing a book.'

'Oh,' her eyes seem to reply. 'That's nice. What's it about?'

'A walk along the River Aire. I'm calling it *Walking On Aire*. Clever, eh? I'm good at puns. I've got an English – '

'Oh! Like *Three Men in a Boat*?'

'Well. It's not the River Thames, there were three of them and I don't have a boat. To mention nothing of the dog. But, apart from that, yes.'

'Please don't put me in your book,' her eyes seem to plead. 'Besides, what have my carnal improprieties got to do with the River Aire? Not that they were improper. Like I say, I'm not kinky. And the feather was just a joke.'

Out of the train station, a sign pointed down an alleyway, directing me to Skipton town centre, so I followed the route between metal fences, cutting through another retail park, onto the main road and yet, with no corresponding sign at the other end, it was a good ten minutes before I realised I was firmly on the road to Keighley, so I turned back.

And it was then, as I trundled along, that I saw the Aire. It was flowing underground, briefly surfacing between Morrisons supermarket and its petrol forecourt. If it was the Aire, it didn't look too well, as if it had fallen into bad company, having turned the colour of turd-brown and doing a cracking impression of sewage. And then, before I knew it, it was off again and out of sight.

I wandered up to the castle and stood outside in two minds. Should I pay to go in? It was over five pounds for adults. If I was writing a travel guidebook (who *are* the masochists who research and write these books, these thick, pocket-sized paperbacks, filled to the brim with information, devoid of personality, humour, opinion, artistic licence, just facts and figures and diagrams and photos and maps?) then I would no doubt feel duty-bound to pay the admission and spend the next hour feigning interest in battlements and flagpoles and the history of the aristocracy who lived in luxury while all those outside the walls lived in anything but. So I would stand there, taking photos, asking the guides relevant questions, or buying an overpriced programme, after paying through the nose for the privilege.

Instead, I went to the British Heart Foundation charity shop on High Street, bought a second-hand DVD *The Unknown Cyclist*, which I would watch on my return home, and set off again in search of my wet and watery quarry.

I like Skipton. Not only is it a lovely town, but also the best bits (castle, church, canal, market), are all within sight of each other. Unlike, say, London, where you've got to hurry through the Tube or along the banks of the Thames, to see the sights. You could be there a month, and you would still not have seen everything. The even bigger difference between the two, of course, is that you can stop someone to ask for directions and they won't shrug you off, or pretend not to hear you, or condescend to help you. Help at Skipton – in fact all along the Aire – was friendly and forthcoming.

Again, I fleetingly caught sight of the Aire, but it suddenly disappeared under a concrete parapet, and was gone again. And so it was to be on this expedition. It was unreasonable to expect it to accompany me on the entire trip. It was obviously a busy river and had other demands on its time. It needed time on its own to recuperate. But then Skipton doesn't need the River Aire. Its pleas to the tourist board for more attention have fallen on waxed-up ears. Skipton has a canal. A castle. A church with a big clock. A solicitors called Savage Crangle. What use is the Aire to a place such as Skipton?

So I allowed the town to play temporary host to me.

I languished on the canal for some time. There was a jazz band playing and a troupe of Morris Dancers doing what Morris Dancers do, and a lazy, relaxed atmosphere. Eventually, I headed off to the next destination. The tourist office advised me to catch the train to Bingley, to avoid the busy road from Skipton, but I walked on, as I wanted to visit other places enroute.

Lack of research may mean an expedition full of surprises, but it can also result in a few deflated balloons. I was particularly looking forward to visiting the village of Kildwick. I had heard of the giant horse made of chalk carved into a hillside here. So I asked a few local residents where the giant horse was or, indeed where the hillside was, as the land seemed pretty flattish in the immediate vicinity, and after a succession of bemused looks and scratched heads, one elderly gentleman suggested I travel to *Kilburn* in North Yorkshire to see *that* giant chalk horse instead. He gave me a condescending glance, as if I were three-quarters stupid, the sort of glance that the rest of us reserve for officials in council buildings, and walked off with a shake of the head and a chuckle.

Fortunately, there was an additional note scribbled in my notebook about a local grave with the name John Laycock added in an almost illegible scrawl. Was this Kildwick or Kilburn?

I flicked through my mental card index. The name did ring a bell, but I hadn't stored it away in any of the important sections of my mind, so as it panicked and careered wildly like a joy rider, through the more dense and unchartered regions of my subconscious, hurriedly looking for something to connect it with, I tried to remember the significance of the name.

Oh dear. Still no joy. But then, just as my brain began making preparations for the psychological equivalent of hari-kari, the name suddenly returned, popping out from one of the dark, shady, cobwebbed alcoves of the mind, which I just use as storage for all the utterly useless bits of information which I'm sure I'll never need – except for the all-important match-points in pub quizzes – and it came to me in a flash.

Of course, I thought. John Laycock! Yorkshire's renowned organist. In the churchyard is his grave, shaped like his favoured instrument. Folk flocked from far and wide to watch him playing with his magnificent organ.

On one of my regular detours away from the river, skirting a road with no pavement (pedestrians prohibited), a car raced up behind me and past me and beeped its horn, which made me jump, and I scrambled to the wall at the roadside, clinging to it like a limpet to a rock. Then, a minute later, the very same car passed on the far side, beeping again. A third time it approached me silently on the near side, this time treating me to a revving engine, just seconds before it roared past, and this time the driver gave a double-beep – 'honk-honk' – like a 'da-dum' on a drum, at the end of some awful pantomime pun. I span round just in time to glimpse the driver's maniacal grin, before he sped off in a puff of exhaust fumes. It had provided sixty seconds of entertainment for him and sixty seconds of life-quickly-flashing-before-my-very-eyes for me. I didn't catch his licence number, or even the make of his car (they all look the same to me, those shiny, mobile coffins, all done out in stitched upholstery and carbon monoxide) but he knows *who* he is and I know *what* he is.

At Cononley, the Aire retreated to private land again with seagulls and a heron languishing on its lazy banks, while I trudged a busy dual carriageway, behind a crash barrier. The road was still wet after heavy rain, and several drivers splashed me, mostly by accident, but a few with vindictive undertones. With every step, the barrier pushed me into the trees bordering the road, the cars choked me with their fumes and the Aire waved merrily from afar, having the time of its life. Connonly turned its nose up at me. It did not want my presence. Nor did it's busy road, or the speeding commuters. I could see the railway line at a distance, as it pointed a mocking finger at me, shouting 'Told you so – there are places where hikers are not destined to go – full of things better not spoken of', but I shouldered on regardless, to Steeton and Silsden. The road bridge, which spanned the railway line, even had its own number: TJC3-768. I may not have the budget (or courage) to trek the globe, but how many of history's great explorers could recite the Steeton/Silsden bridge number? Eat your heart out, Captain Cook. Marco Polo – get a life.

Here, there is a residential area on one side and industry – Brewchem Pipework and Fabrication Industrial Park – on the other, but above that on either side is some gorgeous countryside, amidst a wide-sweeping valley, and there's treasure in them thar' hills. Or at least there was.

A hoard of twenty-seven gold coins was found by metal-detectorist Jeff Walbank in a field in Silsden in 1998. The coins dated from the 1st century and there was also a Roman finger ring, containing a gemstone bearing the figure of a man. What the hoard was worth is not known but it was acquired by Bradford Art Galleries and Museums in 2000, and is now on display at Cliffe Castle Museum in Keighley.

I was looking forward to visiting the village of Utley. I knew nothing about it, other than it rhymes with Muttley. But I completely missed it. As I approached Keighley, the countryside – or what countryside there was amid the buildings and streets - was gradually changing into brooding moorland: jagged rocky outcrops, so characteristic of this wild Pennine landscape; moody and meandering, rough and ready, attractive and frightening in equal measure, like something straight out of *Wuthering Heights* or *The Hound of the Baskervilles*. It's amazing what the tourist board can do with papier-mâché.

Just out of the town centre, I asked for directions to the river. People looked suspicious, then confused, then suspicious again, giving me 'What do you want the Aire for?' looks, as if considering whether or not to report me to the police. For goodness sake, I thought. It's a river. Not the crown jewels. I was walking it. Not looting it.

It became akin to a visual or auditory hallucination. Every time I thought I heard the sound of gushing, tumbling or splashing water, followed with a glimpse of what I took to be running water, it would suddenly pop up in the distance, past a Boots, by a Pizzaland, or through a Sainsburys, and then promptly vanish.

I looked at the map again and could see two long thin blue lines snaking their way through the multitude of motorways, between A-roads and B-roads, suburbs and villages, commons and woods. I studied the map, comparing it to where I was, with the dark blue line signifying the canal, and the lighter blue the Aire, but there was no sign of it.

If I didn't locate it soon, I would sue the cartographers. If they say it's there, then it should be there. The Aire had completely eluded me and I was none too happy. It was all beginning to seem like a one-sided relationship, with me doing all the running around. It had been standoffish with me since Gargrave and I was getting decidedly hacked off.

I took a deep breath and tried to calm myself. This was grave. This was serious. I hadn't felt this cheated since I paid £5.50 to see *Star Wars I: The Phantom Menace*. It didn't seem fair somehow. I had lovingly planned out the trip, done my research, pored over maps, saved up my pennies, travelled all this way. Expeditions like this don't come cheap. Travel any distance in Britain and it costs a wing and a prayer. You can't afford to fart in this country without working overtime.

At this point it dawned on me why so few writers had tackled the Aire for a travelogue. Like me, my fellow scribbling ramblers had probably been seduced by the lure of the snappy title, setting off into the rising sun with new boots and high hopes. And then, very quickly, become disheartened. A lot of the Aire ran under roads and houses, past factories, through private land, along inaccessible shorelines, under bridges, over bridges, to its destination and, in recent years, industrial parks, retail parks and luxury apartment blocks. If it weren't for the towpath of the Leeds & Liverpool Canal as a swish alternative, which I could switch to whenever the river decided to be awkward, then I probably wouldn't be traversing its course now. But I had come this far and so decided I was not giving up. I may not be able to see the river, but it was there on the map, so it had to be out there somewhere.

When all looked lost, a street-sign caught my attention. It read: 'Damside'. I leapt for joy. Dam implied water, water implied river, and river implied River Aire. I'm strong on word association. I have an English degree. Although I could not keep close contact with it, as it darted round the backs of houses and factories, I was just glad we had become re-acquainted, and were moving forward in the same basic direction.

East Riddlesden Hall appeared on the right. Now in the care of the National Trust, it is reputed to be one of the most haunted houses in Yorkshire. Also, a lady I know, Mary Musson, told me that her Great Grandmother, Mary Grange, was born at the Hall, and eventually her and her family became tenant farmers and raised Airedale Heffers. But these are not the only animals bred in the vicinity of the Aire. The Airedale Terrier was originally bred for hunting otters in and around the local valleys.

At Bingley, I lost access to the river, even though it ran behind a row of houses along a busy main road and again I had a choice. Either negotiate my way along the busy dual carriageway, which ran alongside the railway, or stick to the canal. It was not a difficult dilemma. The canal would not lead me too far astray. If I followed the road, I could end up in Bridlington.

I walked past a pub. Some customers were lounging against the wall, others slouched on benches, and one man, who had evidently run the gauntlet by mid-morning, necking too much too soon, was sat on the floor with his head in his hands, mumbling quietly to himself, much to the amusement of the loungers and the slouchers. In South Africa, Doctor Livingstone had a similar experience: 'The boyaloa, or beer of the country, has more of a stupefying effect than exciting nature; hence the beer-bibbers are great sleepers; they may frequently be seen lying on their faces sound asleep.'

Chapter Five

At Saltaire, the river more than made up for its absences on previous stretches, no longer darting in and out of retail parks, dodging through council estates, escaping onto private land, looking dirty and ragged, scuttling down soot-stained passages, between dark and Satanic mills, trying everything in its power to avoid intrepid river explorers such as myself.

Here, the Aire grew into a fully-fledged waterway, with a gushing weir thrown in just for good measure. Strong and lethal, proud and passionate, no longer some neglected, half-nourished cousin of its sister, the Leeds & Liverpool Canal. There was no sense of competition now, as the Aire became smarter and sassier than it had since Malham, not merely polished and neatly-trimmed, dressed in its Sunday best, but positively cosmopolitan, which seemed to reflect the streets, with their pavement cafes and upmarket eateries, and the people, too, who looked thoroughly glad to be there.

It seems that every other industrialist and his dog had set up mills in the centre of Bradford, and many immigrants had arrived from foreign shores to boost its workforce, which made the city absolutely jam-packed. The result, in terms of social hygiene, was disastrous, and the nearby canal (not the Aire) was known locally as the River Stink. A Health Commissioner had deemed Bradford: 'The dirtiest, filthiest and worst regulated town in the kingdom.' But at least I found no derogatory comments about the *people* of Bradford, and so they certainly fared better than those poor souls living in the nearby town of Huddersfield. In 1757, that area was visited by John Wesley who remarked: "A wilder people I never saw in England. The men, women and children filled the streets and seemed just ready to devour us."

What a wimp.

Titus Salt commissioned the local architects Lockwood and Mawson to design his now-famous model village, which would become Saltaire. His new mill was opened in 1853, and by the following year 150 houses were ready for his workforce. Eventually there were 820 houses. Salt wanted to incorporate 'every improvement that modern art and science had brought to light,' including the banning of pubs and, presumably, alcohol. The village included Congregational and Methodist churches, a school, an institute, and a bridge over the mighty River Aire leading to a park. As far as I know, all historians and biographers have praised the life and motivations of Titus Salt and I have found no dissenters. So I will refrain from suggesting that this pioneering industrialist was nothing more than an egomaniacal megalomaniac, affectionately nicknamed Titus A Dux-Ass by his workforce. He may have been, but I have found no evidence for it.

A local tourist leaflet states: 'Forty years before the first state pension, elderly or infirm persons of good 'moral character' were provided with a home and a pension in the Almshouses.' I dare say that elderly or infirm persons who were so poor that they had to steal for a living were not included, and it would be interesting to discover the specific meaning of 'good moral character'. Phrases such as this were often used to denote those who came from well-to-do backgrounds, 'lady' and 'gentleman' merely meant women and men from moneyed families, with the awful and misused word 'respectable' often applied to denote the same. But what were the actual working conditions like, and were the worker's wages up to much? Unfortunately, I have found no written records of the mill workers themselves, and it would be intriguing to learn of their viewpoint too. But, regardless of the working conditions at the mill, there is no doubting Salt's good intentions.

Strange things happen along the River Aire and, while the banks of the River Ganges are populated by all manner of fierce creatures with wide jaws and sharp teeth, ranging from Bengal tigers to the aptly named 'mugger' crocodiles, the Aire is not the sort of place you would expect to find any beastie more fearsome than a squirrel.

However, it was reported in the *Sunday Express* on 6th March 1983, that local man David Bottomley was out walking his collie dog, Sheba, along the riverside at Saltaire, when the collie darted into the bushes to chase a curious-looking creature. The animals engaged in a vicious fight, and Mr Bottomley was unable to separate them. Eventually, the collie killed the other animal. The man peered down at the creature and was puzzled by what he saw. It had a small head, long and thin dog-like muzzle, small rounded ears, long wolf-like fangs and a handsome, silky, snow-white coat. He later identified it by searching through a wildlife book. His dog had killed an Arctic Fox, and a zoologist examined the body later and confirmed it.

Certain parts of Yorkshire are said to be the haunt of so-called Mystery Big Cats. Pumas, panthers, leopards and cougars reportedly stalk the countryside around the Aire, particularly large wooded areas like the one I was currently passing through, just past Esholt. I had seen wild deer before, plus rabbits and foxes, but what would I do if I rounded a bend in a peaceful wooded glade and found a growling black panther blocking my path? Doctor Livingstone survived a near-fatal attack in the African Bush: 'I saw the lion just in the act of springing upon me... Growling horribly, he shook me just as a terrier dog does a rat...'

But what would *I* do, faced with such a creature, with no native bearers armed with guns ready to come to my rescue? What *could* I do, apart from shaking and quaking, amid the putrefying smell of fear, and wishing I had packed a pair of brown trousers?

The next port of call was Baildon and I could find nothing whatsoever to say about the place. I leafed through history books, combed library archives and dived into, and out of, and back into, piles of press cuttings, coming up whole minutes later, gasping for breath. I searched high and low for something interesting to write, even spending a good hour walking up and down the main street, peering at buildings and lampposts and even a passer-by who shouted at me to stop peering at him.

Eventually, I found something in a book called *A History of Yorkshire* by David Hey – and here it is: 'The first Boulton and Watt steam-powered textile mill in Yorkshire was erected at Baildon in 1796 by Cockshott and Halliday.'

Hallelujah! I was determined to discover more. Eventually, I found a pub and darted inside.

'So what's all this I hear about Yorkshire's first-ever

steam-powered textile mill being built in 1796 in Baildon?,'
I asked the packed pub. Or maybe I said something else.

Everyone turned to me and the bar-room murmurs died
away.

'That is to say, not just any old steam-powered textile
mill, but one built by Boulton and Watt.'

Silence.

'Inserted by Cockshott and Halliday', I added for good
measure.

Silence.

I looked around and everyone avoided my gaze. Either
they had all been caught off-guard, forgetting Baildon's rich
past or perhaps they were proud Yorkshire folk, keeping
their cards to their chests and deciding to play it cool.

'Where you from?' asked one man.

'Halifax,' I said.

'Not with an accent like that.'

'I am. From Halifax.'

'With an accent like that? Don't think so.'

I explained – as I always have to explain to people who
have nothing better to talk about than accents – that I had
left the town of my upbringing at the age of twenty-five,
spent three years at Anglia Polytechnic in Cambridge
doing an English degree, spent a few more years on-and-
off working there, and then returned.

'So you're from down south?'

I hate it when people don't listen.

'No. I'm from Halifax. *Up north.*'

'Not with that accent.'

'Say,' came a woman's voice from behind the bar.

'Yes? Hello?' I replied quickly, eager to change the topic.

'You're not local, are you?'

I sighed. 'I am *local*. I'm from Halifax.'

'What – Halifax, *Nova Scotia*?'

The bar erupted in guffaws and chuckles, quickly followed by similar examples of hearty hilarity and scornful merriment.

'No. Halifax, West Yorkshire. Land of the free and plenty.'

Her eyes narrowed and at least twenty other pairs of eyes joined them in suspicious unison, locking on me, like nuclear-powered, heat seeking farts.

'Are you having a pint?' asked the barmaid. 'What do you southerners like to drink?'

I don't know what happened to my Yorkshire accent – if I ever had one. I must have lost it during my years down south. If it had been important to me, I would no doubt have been careful to cherish it, but I could never think of any good reason to do so. What use would it be? Would it help me get a job? My degree certainly didn't.

'So where are you *really* from?' said a man in a chunky cardigan.

I sighed. 'I'm from Halifax.'

'Not with an accent like that.'

For goodness sake, I thought. What's the matter with everyone? Isn't it good enough simply to be human? I did not want a never-ending discussion about my accent – and have to pay for the privilege – so I mumbled something and left.

No doubt everyone in that pub would still be talking about this event in ten years' time.

'Remember when that tall, funny-looking southerner, pretending to be a northerner, came in asking about the Boulton and Watt steam-powered textile mill, inserted by Cockshott and Halliday in 1796? Remember that? Aye. We saw him off, didn't we? He got scared and scarpered. Off like the clappers. Back home with all the other southern pansies.'

Eventually it would become the stuff of legend. The youth of tomorrow would question the middle-aged of today, and say in hushed tones 'did that *really* happen, or is it just a local myth?' and the older patrons would wink knowingly and intriguingly, promising to tell them in return for a pint of Black Sheep's Muff. Perhaps it would even become part of the local heritage, inspiring the composition of Clannad-type folk songs, with children getting a special day off school to commemorate it, and dance gaily around a Southern Nancy-Boy maypole.

As soon as I thought I was never going to discover anything more about Baildon, I was attacked by a low-flying snippet.

Baildon is the birthplace of cricketer Brian Close and Richard Whiteley, of 'Countdown' fame.

I had just ingested this fact when another one flew at me, hurled from a dangerous direction.

The local hall is named after a local climber Ian Clough, who was killed in a tragic accident.

And another.

He used to practice climbing Baildon Bank, an ex-quarry face, with fellow mountaineer Chris Bonnington.

And another.

Baildon Moor was one of the locations for various films including Monty Python's 'The Meaning of Life,' 'Billy Liar' and 'Rita, Sue and Bob, Too.'

Now they were coming thick and fast.

Baildon Moor is also the location of a stone circle called Soldier's Trench, thought to date back to the Bronze Age, some three thousand years ago.

My pen was scribbling the info in my notebook, which was steaming at the speed, as it scrawled across the page.

Baildon was one of the centres for the British Gypsy Community, as far back as 1770. The main street of Baildon bears a monument called the 'Potted Meat Stick', built by one Baron Amphlett, of Somerset, as a memorial to his mother-in-law.

Baildon is also…

'Please, please, no more!' I begged.

And the volley ceased.

Maybe something magical had happened. There was information everywhere I looked, and colourful descriptions popped into my mind at a moment's notice. Was I finally finding my travel writer's feet?

As I walked further along the path, my map informed me that Baildon had turned into Charlestown, though the river and its banks remained unchanged, populated with building sites and a retail park on the near side, and factories on the far side, with wooden pallets and other debris strewn on the slope opposite. The banks of the Aire at Charlestown, as with so many other pleasant backwaters these days, seem to have been mistaken for a rubbish dump, with one of the leisure activities here being fly-tipping. But then – *Eureka!* – I saw the first supermarket trolley of the journey and then, within a hundred yards, there were two more together, as if conjoined, Siamese-style, rusted and mangled, damming the flow.

I considered the river, as it meandered its modest path through the fields, and wondered if it was envious of its more adventurous cousins. At this very moment, I knew that the Wharfe was flowing languidly past Bolton Abbey, and the Derwent was forming a double-act with the Ouse at Barmby-On-The-Marsh. Further on, the Ouse was flowing smartly through York, putting on a show for the tourists, with the Swale following suit at Richmond.

Wouldn't I rather be there? Wouldn't the Aire? I darted a look at the river, searching for signs of envy, but it looked quite content, weaving its wet and watery way.

As I continued along the edge, the route suddenly changed its appearance, looking less like a well-ordered footpath and more like a precarious mountain ledge, the sort of ledge that white hunters have a habit of falling off in those Johnny Weismuller *Tarzan* movies, and the further I trudged along the forbidden river of doom and gloom and of no return, the more the path resembled the set of a disaster movie. Trees from the bank above me were uprooted, victims of recent high winds. Some lay across my path, whilst others on the slope below had crashed into the water.

Further along, I saw a group of young blades, on the opposite bank, throwing stones at an object lodged in the river, which looked like an old petrol can.

As I passed opposite them, they eyed each other, sniggering mischievously and their stones began missing the can and hitting the shore below me. Pretty soon, they were hitting the ground just a few feet away and I decided to press ahead. The stones didn't hit their mark, but they were coming dangerously close, and as I edged further along the bank, the mob edged along to keep up with me. The strange thing is that they didn't seem to be doing it out of maliciousness. It seemed just a game to them and they looked confused as to why I wasn't entering into the spirit of things, joining in the fun, grinning wildly, gamely dodging their missiles, and laughing at their attempts to stone me to death. Never once did it seem to occur to them, that I was not a willing target. That this failed to constitute my idea of fun.

Perhaps I had got it wrong. Maybe they were smiling because it was some strange local custom such as skipping or Morris Dancing which, of course, I would have known about prior to my visit if I hadn't avoided research. But isn't that one of the beauties of travelling into the unknown?

The wonderful and beautiful unpredictability of it all - so different from the repetitive and routine - the path of dead reckoning which seems to define our society, destroying the zest of daily life?

But whether the stone throwing was a traditional custom or not, it was not to my liking, and I looked for a means of escape. My saviour came in the guise of Henry Morton Stanley. On his quest to find Dr Livingstone, the explorer recounted how his expedition came under attack from natives. When his men became fearful, he convinced them to stand their ground and see it through, with nothing more than applying an imposing tone of voice: '...I suddenly shot out my voice with the full power of my lungs, in sharp, quick accents of command to paddle ashore, and the effect was wonderful. It awoke them like soldiers to the call of duty... I have often been struck at the power of a decisive tone, it appears to have an electric effect, riding rough-shod over all fears, indecision and tremor... I had frequently, up river, when the people were inclined to get panic-stricken, or to despair, restored them to a sense of duty by affecting the sharp-cutting, steel-like, and imperious tone of voice, which seemed to be as much of a compelling power as powder to a bullet.'

So it was, I decided there and then to adopt a decisive tone to halt these hoodlums, but on looking back a second later, they had vanished. Perhaps I had overdosed on chocolate and hallucinated it all. Or perhaps the mere thought of Stanley's influence had scared them away. I felt myself in good company.

A hundred yards on, the path opened out into a nicely designed area, with fences, a pool with reeds and a picnic area. This is Denso Marston nature reserve, with a sign near the pool explaining what types of wildlife frequent the area. I found the location surprising, since there was a warehouse just a few feet away. A man on a forklift was stacking pallets, with just a wooden fence separating the two worlds. Nature and industry co-existing. I like the idea and hope it catches on. There was another fence blocking off a small area of trees, but planks of wood had been plucked out at different eye-levels, and at first glance it looked like they had been vandalised, but as I peered through the narrow gaps at the protected trees and watched birds pop in and out of miniature tree houses, I realised it was a twitchers' area. A birdwatchers' paradise.

Just then, I caught sight of an elderly man in a camouflage jacket in the bushes. I'm always suspicious about men who dress in military gear – who are not in the military. Maybe they applied to join the army, got rejected, and never quite recovered from it, and so were resigned to a life of skulking in bushes and feigning a frankly unhealthy interest in shrubbery. But this man had a pair of binoculars. He was either a bird-watcher or a Peeping Tom. Or both.

He glanced at the birdwatching fence, the pool with reeds, and the birds in the trees, and said: 'I don't understand how anyone cannot be interested in wildlife.'

It's easy, I thought. You start with a distinct lack of interest. Then continue indefinitely. I decided to impress him with exciting details of my expedition, whilst exercising a bit of ego.

'I'm walking the River Aire, boldly going where man has gone before.'

'Sun'll be out later this afternoon.'

I sighed. It is said that the British – and Yorkshire folk in particular – are the most difficult people in the world to impress.

So I tried a different tack.

'I've built a time machine and am planning to wing my way through the centuries, have tea and bikkies with Boadicea and be back in time for *Bodger and Badger.*'

'Aye. Nice weather for it.'

We paused a moment, enjoying the gentle birdsong, surrounding foliage and afternoon aesthetics.

Suddenly, he said: 'I've been walking around the Aire, fifty years, man and boy.'

'Bet you've seen the river change,' I said. 'Bet you've witnessed the many changes in the flow of the river.'

The man nodded, smiling wistfully, as if remembering brighter and happier times, the golden days of his youth, in his long association with the River Aire, during which it had no doubt seen many, many, changes.

'Aye,' I said. 'I bet you've seen it change. As all things change. As nothing remains the same. As nothing in the space-time continuum remains the same. Aye. I bet you've seen the river change.'

The man nodded again, turned to me, and said: 'No. Not really.'

So we stood there awhile.

After a brief pause, we tried another awhile, but couldn't recreate the intensity of the first one. Sequels are never as good, and I became quite disillusioned with them after that.

'Y'know,' he said. 'Some folk believe there's a Guardian of the River Aire.'

'And is there?'

'Of course not. Don't be daft. There's no such thing. In fact, some even call *me* the Guardian of the Aire.'

'Why would they call you that?'

'Well, I must look like I hope they might.'

'Oh,' I said. 'And what do you tell them?'

'I tell them not to be daft. There's no such thing.'

He shook his head, took a deep breath, cocked a leg, and let out a trumpeting fart, which scared some birds in a nearby tree. Then he bid me good day, and disappeared into the trees, from whence he came.

I sat on one of the benches, took out my packed lunch, and glanced through a booklet I picked up which told me about Yorkshire rivers and the various active pursuits which can be enjoyed in their proximity. I found a whole page dedicated to the subject of picnics and – would you believe – picnic poems. This is a category of literature, which never once cropped up on my English degree. It begins with a poem by Thomas Wharton:

Their weary spirits to relieve
The meadows' incense breathe at eve
No riot mars the simple fare
That o'er a glimmering hearth they share.

'It's fun dreaming up a picnic menu,' the booklet claims – which I find amazing. Call me obtuse – and many people do – but you could sit me down with a pen and notebook (from now until the day when an infinite number of monkeys would sufficiently evolve to produce the works of Shakespeare) and tell me to make a list of all the things in life from which one could derive fun, and it would never once occur to me to rank 'dreaming up picnic menus' as one of them.

The booklet includes an apparent picnic poem dating from 1690 by famous diarist Samuel Pepys:

...a dish of marrow-bones; a leg of mutton; a loin of veal; a dish of fowl; three pullets and two dozen of larks all in a dish; a great tart, a neat's tongue, a dish of anchovies, a dish of prawns, and cheese.

That's not a poem. It's a shopping list. It's a good job old

Sammy Peeps stuck to writing diaries instead of picnic poems, because I don't think he would have been as fondly remembered as he is today.

If you have just discovered a new passion in life – reading picnic poems – then I'm very happy for you, but the exercise has been totally lost on me.

Though perhaps I'm being cynical. Maybe it is fun – ridiculously enjoyable fun – to dream up a picnic menu and maybe it is, indeed, a jolly good hoot to quote from relevant literary gems, such as classic and world-renowned picnic poems.

But now I'm getting giddy, so better to move on.

Chapter Six

Just out of Charlestown, I was eager to get off the road and back to the water, but the more I walked, the further the road began to veer away from the river. I considered retracing my steps and back down the footpath to the nature reserve, until I happened upon Esholt Lane, which jutted off towards said waterway.

Suddenly, I heard something and strained my ears to listen. The sound of running water! I realised that the Aire must be close by. Either that, or the leaves were splashing in the trees.

In a field adjoining a house, I spotted a horse. A spotted horse in fact. No doubt an exotic hybrid. Zebra crossbred with cheetah.

A tiny river, too minor to be honoured with a name, flowed through a farm and under a humped bridge I was crossing, and joining the Aire, which appeared beside me, like the shopkeeper in Mister Benn, as if by magic. I passed the Old Barn pub and restaurant, with golf range attached to it, and passed a couple of caravan parks. Then I found the Aire, but there was no obvious access, no footpath on the nearside, just a muddy bank, and no bridge to reach the other side, so I kept on the road to Esholt. This village is where they filmed parts of the TV series Emmerdale.

My friend Silvie phoned from Cambridge and I told her about Esholt and the Emmerdale connection. She asked for a souvenir, so I bought her a Zak Dingle key-ring from the village shop.

'Get many tourists in here?' I asked the shopkeeper.

'That's £1.50, please.'

I handed the money over.

'Many tourists pass through?'

'Thankyou,' he said, indicating business was done, and nodding his head to the door, just in case I'd forgotten where it was. Stupid question, really. Of course there were tourists. Why else would anyone come here by the coach load? Not that there's anything wrong with the place.

I went to the pub – the Woolpack – and ordered a pot of tea. The walls were adorned with photos of the cast such as Annie Sugden? Seth? Amos? (sorry, don't do soaps).

As I sat outside, drinking tea and smoking a roll-up, an elderly man with wild hair and a chequered dressing gown, who looked like his name might be Sir Reginald Klinkers, came out of his house, emptied a rubbish bag in a wheelie bin and gave me a beady look. I had no desire for a beady look at that time, so I threw it back at him as he returned indoors.

I searched high and low for a way to escape Esholt and return to the river but, once again, it had gone off on its own, proving inaccessible. All I could do was peer through the trees to see it skulking off along the valley, with the land on each shore blocked off with either barbed wire or impenetrable foliage. The river ventured through more private land, prostituting itself to owners of country cottages and penthouse apartments, skirting their properties and marketing itself as an attractive landscape feature.

I followed the road up through the village, past a coach park, under a viaduct and back to the main road, as it veered off up the hill to God-knows-where (Guiseley, as it turned out) and there was nothing for it, but to call it a day and make a note to return to Baildon on my next visit, but to cross to the opposite side of the river.

And so it was, some days later that I queued for the Baildon bus at Bradford Interchange. An elderly lady shuffled past, peered at the sign on the bus and looked up at me.

"Baildon?"

"Sorry?"

"Baildon bus."

I pointed to the sign on the bus, which read 'Baildon'.

"Yes. Baildon bus."

"Bus to Baildon?"

"Bus to Baildon. Yes."

"Says Wyke."

"Sorry?"

"Says Baildon via Wyke."

I looked at the sign on the bus.

"Yes," I confirmed. "Bus to Baildon via Wyke."

"Not usually."

"Sorry?"

The woman sighed, as if one of us wasn't making a lot of sense. Which was true. I just hoped it wasn't me.

"Baildon bus goes through Towngate, not Wyke."

"Right."

"What?"

"Yes." I said, feeling decidedly uncomfortable, at the prospect at another pointless conversation.

"It does."

"Sorry?"

"Baildon. Via Wyke. Not Towngate. Usually."

"Hmmm," I nodded my head, smiled, did both at once, then hoped the driver would open the doors and let me escape more of this verbal ba-ba. I like to seek discourse on my expedition. Conversations with people I would not otherwise have met. But you have to draw the line somewhere.

And so I alighted the bus on the bridge over the Aire at Baildon, and set off trudging along the other side. I ducked down an alleyway – dead end. Another one – dead end. Eventually, I got on the canal towpath, and followed it through yet another industrial park, until the surroundings became quiet and the pace unhurried.

Despite my failure to find anything much to say about Baildon-by-the-Aire, I certainly found something to say about Baildon-by-the-Canal. Although it was late September, the sun was out and it was warm, just like July. This was one of the prettiest and peaceful stretches since Malham. The river was on my left (somewhere) and, between us, an increasing amount of impenetrable foliage, and the railway to my right. A swan was preening itself in one of those pointless mirror-windows that office blocks have. A house past the railway had a Union Jack on a flagpole flapping in the breeze. Dragonflies were zooming through the air in singles, or waltzing in twos. They were either dancing or fighting or mating, but I wasn't close enough to determine which. A swan and some ducks looked nervous as I approached, but they gave me the benefit of the doubt and it paid off.

There is some great woodland here. Dark under the leaves, but with occasional shafts of sunlight penetrating the dense foliage, no doubt designed by some greater power to inspire the heart to sing in short melodic bursts.

Of course, my initial trip through Baildon and Charlestown had skirted the main road, flanked by residential and industrial – not an area's most attractive side at the best of times – but the current location, the towpath on the canal, was shrouded from the road, and the residents - the Bailies and the Charleys – were obviously keeping schtumm about this jewel in the county's crown – and who could blame them? I had certainly been too critical of Baildon and Charlestown. What a great place to spend a summer's day. Any day, in fact.

During her African journey, Mary Kingsley paddled her canoe into the middle of a lake to meditate, and she described how the power of Africa surrounded her and how she surrendered herself to its influence. She wrote: 'Do not imagine that it gives rise in what I am pleased to call my mind, to those complicated, poetical reflections (which) nature seems to bring out in other people's minds. It never works that way with me; I just lose all sense of human individuality, all memory of human life, with its grief and worry and doubt, and become part of the atmosphere. If I have a heaven, that will be mine.'

And mine, at least so far, was the canal between Baildon and Charlestown. I felt relaxed, warm and happy. It was one of those moments when you feel like the entire world's problems can bugger off just for a while and leave you in vacant peace. For that moment, life is intensely satisfying, where there's nothing to think or worry about. There's nothing to do or see, leaving you time just to be.

I peered to my left and thought I could see the road through Esholt curving up to the main thoroughfare, towards the noise of Guisley, but whilst here, I was in a walkers, bikers and anglers paradise.

I stopped by a sign: Ainsbury Avenue. I looked around

and scratched my head, confused. I couldn't see any turn-offs; certainly no avenue, or crescent, or lane as such. Not even a measly cul-de-sac. No highways at all. Just a sign saying Ainsbury Avenue. Strange.

Nearby was a forlorn bridge, made of girders, and I scrambled up a track to explore. One side led to a padlocked gate blocking the way, which was pretty pointless, since beyond that was a steel fence, surrounded by barbed wire, coming from nowhere and leading nowhere. What lay behind it, I wondered, which required such high-level security? King Kong? Jurassic Park? The bridge led to the other side of the canal, the highly enticing woodland, and I was tempted to follow it, trading sun for shade, but I remembered I was following the Aire, and was already some way from it, so returned to the towpath.

I reached a lock on the canal, and two narrow boats and their crews were negotiating their way through. Two young lads were angling on the opposite side. Two older lads, German by the sounds of it, were fishing further down. In fact, as I walked on, I saw several anglers on the canal and I peered at them, trying to catch their eye, which would serve as an invitation for me to ask questions about their hobby, but they took great care to avoid my eye-catching ambitions. Conversation alerts the fish and all the anglers wanted was a bit of peace and quiet, away from the hustle and bustle of the populated areas and safe from the inquisition of a wayward writer.

There are several different types of fishing, (including *Fly Fishing* by J. R Hartley), but the two main types, as far as I know, are coarse and game. Fishing for salmon and trout was regarded as a gentlemen's sport. They were considered more palatable – and therefore gastronomically superior – than the others, so the quest for them became known as 'game' fishing. Thus salmon and trout joined the ranks of other palatable wildlife such as grouse, gracing well-heeled dinner tables. The other varieties – barbel, bream, common carp, chub, tench, eel, goldfish, perch, pike, roach, rudd and zander were considered 'unpalatable' and therefore not highly sought by the upper echelons. Hence the term 'coarse'. So, as it turns out, the difference between coarse and game is simply a matter of taste. Which was news to me. I thought game fishing was for the sociable sort, who do it with friends, horse around, have a few beers and a bit of a giggle, while coarse fishing was where you do it on your own, swearing under your breath, and fondling yourself when you think no-one's looking. This expedition was becoming a real education.

Unwanted by the anglers, and anyone else, I sat on a bench and rolled a fag. A memorial plaque read: 'In loving memory of Arnold, Sheila and Margaret Fairs.' I longed to know more about them. How had they spent their lives? Why a memorial to all three? And why here? With no pending conversation with the living, I was desperate to form a link with the dead. Travel isn't just about places, but about people, and I longed for some human contact. But the dead don't talk and neither do benches or plaques. I did pass various people further along my route. But several ignored me and the few who glanced and smiled, glanced and smiled in a way which said, 'yes, I've seen you, but please don't engage me in conversation, it's a nice day, a nice place, don't spoil it by talking.' Besides, I couldn't think of anything to say that would give me an excuse to talk to them. My brother, who used to smoke, once went on holiday on his own, purposefully without a cigarette lighter. This gave him a reason to go and talk to people, to make conversation, if only briefly, to ask for a light. I could do the same of course, but everyone I passed looked far too sensible to smoke, too energetic and too full of life to actively seek an artificial stimulant like nicotine.

At the Esholt Waste Water Treatment Works, a sign included a photo-montage of how the plant looked now, and how it was going to look later, with a before-and-after shot of the sewage works, for the benefit of graduates in human wastage, with a numbered diagram explaining which parts of the plant were going to deal with which types of poop, and how micro-organisms feed on the 'stuff' that they process and… I paused and turned away. Someone has to study sewage and classify different types of 'grades' or 'varieties' of it, and re-construct sewage plants and design holding chambers for it all, and I'm glad someone does, but I'm glad it's not me.

So I walked on. After a mile or so, the woods seemed to melt away, replaced with farm fields on the left, and to the right was some lovely countryside sloping up towards who-knows-where, and a little way past that were some posh-looking houses, like a concrete utopia, if that's not a contradiction in terms. The canal had suddenly gone upmarket. Smart wooden black & white rails separated the footpath from the canal. This was Apperley Bridge Marina, populated by a mass of well-heeled narrowboats, like a Yorkshire Riviera.

Turning off the bridge, I stopped at a café. For eighty-pence, I got a giant mug of tea and sat outside in the shade of the awning. Why I don't sensibly drink ice-cold drinks on sweltering days I don't know, but I do like a hot cup of cha-cha.

As soon as I sat down, the staff began to put the chairs on the tables, wipe down the place mats, and generally look as if they were closing up, which I considered a bit of a cheek.

Although they said nothing, I got the distinct impression they wanted me to sip up and ssip off.

Afterwards, I visited a football ground: Cragg Bridge United, where a schoolboys' game was going on. A group of burly men with skinheads eyed me as I walked through the gates, one of them with the obligatory pit bull (Status symbol? Fashion accessory? Wouldn't leave home without it?) and then returned my friendly smile, flatly refusing to be socially stereotyped by any cynical travel writer who happened to pass their way.

I made a note of the number on the bridge nearby: C 341 A. Why? I honestly don't know. I felt that it might come in handy at some point. Maybe I would find myself in a pub quiz and victory would rest on one of those questions that nobody can answer but me: Name all the actors who played *The Magnificent Seven*? (Yul Brynner, Steve McQueen, James Coburn, Charles Bronson, Robert Vaughan – and the two they always forget – Horst Bucholtz and Brad Dexter). Who played the bandit Calverro in the same movie and also the 'ugly' in *The Good, The Bad and The Ugly*? (Eli Wallach). Which other film featured McQueen, Coburn and Bronson? (*The Great Escape*). Name *all* of the seven dwarfs (Doc, Grumpy, Dopey, Sleepy, Sneezy, Bashful and Happy). What is the number of the bridge at Apperley Bridge, as noted in that classic and incredibly amusing travelogue *Walking On Aire*? (C 341 A)

Back on the canal, I found a metal sign, with the top bit resembling two boomerangs stuck together. The words engraved on the front revealed this as being funded by the Royal Bank of Scotland; one of a thousand signs to mark the creation of the National Cycle Network, by the organisation Sustrans. The Network began as a 17-mile traffic-free trail on the former Bristol and Bath Railway, intended for the use of walkers and cyclists. In 1995, funding of £43.5 million from the Millennium Commission Lottery Grant was used to convert disused train tracks into similar paths – and 12,000 miles of such routes existed throughout Britain by 2007. As if to emphasise this, four hairy and muddy cyclists whizzed past – the Hell's Angels of mountain biking.

Further on, a roguish looking character was cycling a rickety bike up and down the towpath. I guessed he had fished it from the canal or the river and was hoping to repair it and sell it on somewhere. His narrowboat, tethered to the towpath, was amazing, covered in odds and ends, bits and bobs, which he had also no doubt fished out of the water at various points. He appeared to be a canal tinker. A waterborne Womble. Making good use of the things that he finds, things that the everyday folk leave behind. The bike he was riding was tiny – obviously a child's bicycle – and he looked distinctly comical on it, as he was large and robust, big enough to be both Steptoe *and* Son. He wore what looked like a pirate's headscarf, reminding me of an older version of Johnny Depp's character Captain Jack Sparrow, with a Dead Man's Chest and a belly to match, after a yo-ho-ho and too much rum. I smiled at him, tried to catch his eye, but he completely ignored me. As a travel writer, this is exactly the sort of person I needed to be talking to, so that people would read my book and think: 'Wow! What an interesting life this Owens character seems to have! He always meets such fascinating folk!'

A signpost told me that Rodley was three miles away, and Leeds was a whopping nine-and-a-half miles, while Shipley was four miles, (had I only walked *four* miles?) and Bingley seven miles.

I came to a bridge across the canal, and for the first time on the expedition there was graffiti: a love heart followed by the words 'Slapper Spice'. Gone were the high fences and sewage works guarded by barbed wire. On the left, large buildings in the distance, scary and sandblasted, like the Barratt Homes version of Colditz, and beside me were huge rocks acting as seats for the weary adventurer, weighing down the neatly mowed grass flanking the canal.

A signpost announced that I had reached a place called Calverley Bridge, and giving a history of the area. It mentioned something called fulling mills and scribbling mills. I don't know what the first one means, but the latter sounds like a school for creative writing.

I peered through the bushes to my left and the Aire, a few minutes ago nowhere to be seen, was now in full flow, still inaccessible, but still undeniably there. A lengthy stretch of companionship had made us both too clingy, in each other's pockets. We had needed a break and were now back together, fully refreshed. We regaled each other with our different adventures while we had been apart. The Aire told of the funny people it had flowed past, the sights and sounds of the life of a backwater river, while I waxed lyrical about the Jonny Depp look-alike and the Yorkshire Riviera. I thought this conversation was actually going on in my imagination, until a hefty chap in a 'I'm-a-lumberjack-and-I'm-OK' shirt, sporting a rucksack and walking boots, who looked like his nickname at school might have been Porky Stinky-Pants, approached me and said: 'It's only a river, you know. You can't converse with them, like you can with a person. You can talk to it, but it won't reply. If you keep muttering to yourself you are liable to end up in a straitjacket.'

I disagreed with him. You can converse with a river. Not

verbally, but spiritually perhaps, and that's what I had been doing. I just didn't realise I had been doing it aloud.

'Don't listen to him,' the Aire whispered to me, in that non-verbal way that only mystical rivers of the mind can whisper. 'He's just jealous. He's spent a lifetime walking up and down this waterway. I've seen him before, struggling along, desperately seeking a way to connect with the natural world in some deep and spiritual way. But he can't. And you can. He's jealous. Ignore him.'

Later I arrived at Kirkstall Abbey. A leaflet stated that the Cistercians established the Abbey in 1152 after an aborted start at record-breaking Barnoldswick. Kirkstall was not plundered at the Dissolution and remains the outstanding example of Cistercian architecture from the Norman period.

Well, I never.

You can enter the grounds through a Visitors Centre, and there are notice boards attached to the walls of the ruins explaining what each part of the Abbey was used for. All important meetings and decisions were taken in the Chapter House. And this is where the monks used to confess to their sins, too, which included sitting by the log fire – longer than they were permitted – during the freezing winters! After meals, they would pray, and the monks were encouraged to make crosses from their breadcrumbs, to stop their minds wandering from the subject of the reading.

I sat on the grass at the Abbey for a while. There was a clearing at the trees, an idyllic spot, where one could sit and watch the river tumble past. Perhaps the Congo or Nile may have been well out of my league, with its lions and tigers and killer crocs, but then I couldn't see the cannibalistic Fang Tribe of West Africa, resplendent in loincloths, thriving on the banks of the River Aire either. The perennial British chill would soon finish them off, and any survivors wouldn't last two minutes trying to cross the busy A65 road alongside the Abbey enroute to Leeds, with lorries and buses rumbling past, molesting the peace of the Abbey grounds and its flow-by river.

Chapter Seven

The whole atmosphere changed as I trudged into the centre of Leeds, the people boasting such vibrant individuality, which comes with life in large settlements, where folk vigorously do their own thing and worry not about gossiping tongues and twitching curtains. People are more concerned with themselves, and spend less time worrying about who is hurrying past them, what they are wearing and what colour hair they have.

And the river became less self-conscious, too. Here, as it flowed under the vast train station, it became a real waterway, wide and blue, giving the canal a real run for its money, as it snaked past the gleaming office blocks and luxury apartments scraping the sky, amid the perpetual noise of one sort or another.

Mary Kingsley wrote: 'Woe to the man in Africa who cannot stand perpetual uproar. Few things surprised me more than the rarity of silence and the intensity of it when you did get it. Every night in the jungle, a terrible cacophony begins.'

It was refreshing to be in a city centre, after so much quiet on my expedition. It's good to be solitary once in a while, where you can hear your own thoughts. But thoughts alone can drive you insane with the incessant chattering of the mind, and it is good to be able to block the transmission once in a while, listening to something louder and more robust.

The sounds of the city came thick and fast. Although they were random, this cacophony could have been a symphony. The car-horns trumpeted a staccato, as the brakes on a bus screeched like a bad violinist, both set against the Hi-NRG, rhythmic bass line of the timpani trains rumbling over tracks at the station nearby.

Hey! I thought. That's quite good. And I scribbled it in my tattered notebook. In fact, it wasn't just good but also rather clever – the sort of Eureka moment that all writers look for. I chuckled to myself and looked up. People were staring. They were probably wondering who this mad git was, rocking back and forth, cackling madly to himself, like a wild-eyed lunatic on an outing from an institution. But let them, I thought. They were probably jealous. Purveyors of self-contained and contrived travel comedy always have a hard time parading their wares to a philistine world.

As I walked along the main street from the station, in the direction which I believed the Aire to be moving, I spied two skinheads, like bollards in Levis, loitering the precinct, glaring at me, eager to misinterpret my casual glance as provocation, a legal loophole – 'If was his fault, officer. He was giving us the evils' – offering them just cause to beat me to a pulp, and escape judicial retribution, due to coming from a poor background, as if that justifies gratuitous violence.

On the precinct, there were pigeons, those aimless wanderers, pecking at the detritus of the shopper, traveller, commuter. Like writers, forever searching for a purpose in life, or at least a purpose slightly more worthy than the last few purposes they have recently flung aside in frustration, sure that there is something more edible and satisfying and meaningful round the next corner. It occurred to me this was the first time I had seen pigeons on the entire expedition. Ever seen a pigeon in the countryside? No, me neither. Pigeons have been with us for decades. They are urban scavengers. Tired of fighting ducks for bread and crows for seeds, their ancestors flew to towns and cities on a whim – and never left. They settled in. Spread the good word. Joined the rat race – but avoided the jobcentre. They have to eat, but don't pay rent. Life is easier for wildlife in the towns. Like David Lodge said in his novel Nice Work: 'Nature is joining the human race and going on the dole.' Perhaps they're paving the way for other species. Foxes and herons are no strangers to the city. What next? Falcons? Hawks? Mystery Big Cats? Fully subscribed devotees of urban materialism, queuing up at the back entrance of the McDonalds and Burger King chemical soup-kitchens.

I knew there would be no more jungle trading posts the size of Leeds after I left the city, so I would need to buy more supplies to last the remainder of the expedition. The great explorers always stocked up with food, but sometimes this wasn't enough.

In his early days, Amundsen joined the Belgian Antarctic Expedition to study the South Magnetic Pole, but the ship became trapped in the winter ice. Stuck there for an incredible thirteen months, two of the crew went mad, (only two?) and the entire crew went down with scurvy, including the Captain. But Amundsen saw this as an early opportunity to take the initiative and assert himself as a leader. As he saw it, the scurvy outbreak was caused, to an extent, by the lack of fresh meat. He turned to the medical officer for advice, before deciding to add penguin and seal meat to everyone's diet. Recovery was dramatic. Little wonder that he always laid such importance on the supply of fresh meat on future expeditions.

Amundsen also had high regard for dogs. And these weren't the friendly fluffy-puppy variety who run to fetch sticks and unravel Andrex toilet rolls, but Eskimo dogs, '…little more than half-tamed wolves, able to withstand the most terrible conditions of ice and snow. Six of them could pull a loaded sledge over the snow-covered wastes of Antarctica, twenty miles away. Six of them also represented 300 lbs of fresh meat.'

Huh?

'Twenty-four of our brave and faithful companions were marked out for death.'

Although Amundsen was never going to be as fondly remembered as Captain Scott, whom he beat in the race to the South Pole, the thing that really turned the British against him, was the slaughtering of the dogs. And this couldn't be described as a 'spur of the moment' decision. Amundsen had coldly and logically decided to kill and eat them two years prior, when he was planning out every detail of his expedition. He even chose the place where he and his comrades would perform the dog-dirty deed, marking it on the map and christening the exact location with the name 'Butchers'.

To eat dogs, even the ferocious Eskimo variety, was deemed as revolting. To enjoy it was considered even worse. Bloodthirsty even. And the explorers did enjoy it – perhaps too much for fair-playing, good-sporting and animal-loving British society. Amundsen's diary entry which read: '…the next day we treated ourselves to dog cutlets… it was excellent, absolutely excellent,' was the last nail in the glory coffin, and the explorer has been widely disregarded in certain circles ever since.

As for myself, I drew the line at fresh meat - or at least the sort of fresh meat that could breathe and walk and run and transport my luggage, just prior to the point that I consumed it – but I took Amundsen's cue and bought an extra supply of Snickers to guard against an outbreak of scurvy.

When Humboldt and Bonpland arrived in Venezuela on 16th July 1799, half of the ship's crew had come down with typhoid, but even this did not diminish their excitement. Humboldt wrote how: '...great palms rose from the shore; clouds of pink flamingos took off from the water. The extravagant sounds and colours were intoxicating. Our excitement on landing was enormous. This was the moment I had dreamt of ever since my first tutor read me his translation of Robinson Crusoe! What a wealth of observation I shall collect here on the earth's construction. What happens lies before me. I am dizzy with joy.'

It would be interesting to know what the pair would make of Hunslet. There were extravagant sounds and colours to be heard and seen here too, and they were certainly intoxicating, if that's the right word, but they didn't leave me dizzy with joy. In fact, as I left the river and took to suburban streets, skirting a busy dual carriageway, the exhaust fumes were making me dizzy with something quite different. But of course this could be said about almost anywhere these days. In fact, as I'd expected, most of the suburbs I passed through looked indistinguishable from one another.

So I stopped and studied the road map. As to be expected, the centre of Leeds was represented as a big sludge of browny-red, covering the city centre and its sprawling suburbs. I could not make head-nor-tail of the mass of highways, twisting and twirling, around and past, through and above and beyond the River Aire.

I didn't fancy trudging through any more of them, stopping and studying the map every few minutes, realising that I should have turned right instead of left, then having to re-trace my steps and locate a different route, finding that the winding streets and terraces did not lead to the next stage of the river as promised. If I entered this maze, I may never re-emerge on the other side. So I decided to cheat – and treat (myself). I would catch a train to the next major destination – Castleford – and cut out all the bits in-between.

There is a sunken barge here, stuck in the weir, directly beneath the bridge. Had a hardy band of intrepid explorers been ambushed by natives armed with blowpipes? No, as it happens. Some local vandals had let it loose during a storm in 1977, and it span down the river before becoming lodged on the weir – where it has remained ever since. The artist Ray Weston drew twenty-four illustrations of the vessel – christened 'Thomas the Barge' – which were put on display in a local art gallery. I bet Stanley and Livingstone didn't know that. Now, I'm not praising vandalism here but, if anything, the sunken barge is an intriguing and fascinating feature of the river. It certainly intrigued and fascinated me.

On the road out of the town centre, there are smart seating areas, and parts cut out of the foliage, so local residents and workers from nearby companies, can sit in fine weather and enjoy the wooded area overlooking the river. I pass the stadium of the Castleford Tigers, with the adjoining rugby ground and a company called The Rock Factory.

The Millennium Bridge is certainly not the only evidence of regeneration in Castleford. On the road to New Fryston, as there is a current restoration of the former Fryston and Wheldale colieries. There is a 'Fresh Aire Regeneration Programme,' reading '10 Years On – National Coalfield Developments' with various paths leading off from the main road, promising evidence of new projects. I want to follow them all, but don't have the time. At the side of the road, obscured by bushes, stands the Wheldale Colliery Memorial – not only to those miners who lost their lives in the pit, but doubling for those local men who died while serving in the Second World War.

I got a bus from a bus stop on the way to New Fryston, planning to get off at Ferrybridge. But I missed it. Quite *how* I missed it, I don't know, since Ferrybridge is famous for having gigantic cooling towers spewing out mushroom clouds of filth into the o-zone – and before I knew it, I was in Knottingley.

Nearly everyone on the street was briskly heading towards and past me. Even the clouds were scurrying in the opposite direction as if there was something happening on the outskirts – a festival or fete – and everyone had a ticket but me. Come hell or hot water, I could not locate the river anywhere. It had goosed me again. I asked for directions and spent the next two hours wandering round in circles and triangles and dodecahedrons. But eventually, I caught sight of it. Unfortunately, there was no access and I had to follow the road, as the Selby Canal (the successor to the Leeds and Liverpool) was piddling around in the distance and – not surprisingly – on its way to Selby, which was miles off my desired route. So I set off plodding down the street.

Just as I was getting into my stride, making progress,

God started spitting. Then he started doing something else, because it began drizzling, and the incessant drumming of the rain on the top of my hood started to drive me crackers. Just as I was nearing the last leg of my expedition – and my tether – Mother Nature was lobbing the elements at me, as if she didn't want me to complete it. And then, to top it all, I came up against another part of the Aire blocked off from the earnest expeditionary, as the road turned away. I felt much like Edmund Blackadder did, when he exclaimed: 'Yet again the devil farts in my face.'

And so my expedition had turned out thus. Get bus or train to point A. Walk to point B. Find a fence or private land or other obstacle blocking my path to point C. Consult map to find alternative route to point C. Arrive at Point C. Walk to point D. Then find path to point E blocked off. Consult map to find alternative route to point E. And so on, and so forth. My expedition was all stops and starts, with no real progress, no multiple miles, no respectable distance made on any single trip. Just when the going seemed to get going, it stopped getting going, and started getting *not* going, in virtually every direction except the one I wanted to get going.

So there and then I made a decision. Stop this larking around, and leave it for today. Forget the route from Knottingley towards East Yorkshire. Instead, I would return in a week, get a train to Goole, a bus to Airmyn, make my way to the end of the River Aire, then double-back and cover the villages I had not yet visited. I prefer to do things in chronological order, and follow maps in cartographical order, but after so many stops and starts – mainly stops – it was time to take drastic action.

Chapter Eight

So it was, a week later, I found myself on the train from Halifax, changing once at Leeds, again at Brough, then onto Goole. As I settled into my seat, a voice came on the intercom. The person it belonged to sounded rather unwell, hoarse and bunged up, as if suffering from Swine Flu, Bird Flu and One Flu (over the cuckoo's nest). He or she – I couldn't tell which – said: 'Please familiarise yourself with the location of Emergency Exits.'

I scoured the carriage, expecting them to be hidden in some way, perhaps disguised as bookcases like the entrance to the Bat Cave. Special exits only to be used in special emergencies. Perhaps a ladder, which pulled down from the ceiling, leading through a specially designed gap in the skylight. Or a button that would flip my seat backwards like Sweeney Todd's deadly barber's chair. Or even those pointless electronic seats in *Thunderbirds*, which transport Scott, Virgil and Brains from one side of the room to the other. But I could see no sign of them, so they must have been cleverly and secretly constructed; obscured from view.

'If in doubt about the location of Emergency Exits, please ask the conductor.'

So I asked the conductor, who gave me a pitying look and pointed to the door I had just entered to board the train.

At Goole, I realised I was close to the sea – or at least the river bit which flows into the sea. It had a seaside air to it, and a big white circular structure, which dominated the skyline. It had the general look and feel of a lighthouse – but was not a lighthouse, as it was far too wide and cumbersome. Stood next to it was a tall, brown, thin tower, which looked like a factory chimney. As I discovered, these were water towers – locally dubbed the 'salt and pepper pots' - and vaguely resembling Laurel and Hardy.

The birds had changed too. There were no crows out here. All the feathered flappers I could see were seagulls, with their dive-bombing swoops accompanied by those characteristic cackles, and although Goole is not the most beautiful town, it felt good at last to be within a few miles of the sea, for it is not that far from Hull. The people, too, looked generally happier and healthier. Even the depressed ones. Even the ones shuffling along pavements and precincts, across roads, in and out of shops and pubs. I considered this extra brightness and sparkle in expressions and complexions to be linked in some way to the proximity of the sea, and its regular breezes – chilly but refreshing – which steal inland without warning and catch you unawares, blowing away the blues.

There was no bus station at Goole, so I asked for directions to the nearest thing resembling one and found a cluster of bus stops on a street wedged between a Lidls and a Wetherspoons. As there was no bus to Airmyn for an hour, I decided to look for a café to escape the chilly weather. There's nothing quite like a cup of tea to warm the spirits of the weary explorer.

Henry Morton Stanley certainly agreed. He wrote: 'I am

like an old woman. I love tea very much and take a quart and a half without any inconvenience. That tea is all our refreshment. It is our beer, our champagne, our wine; and after the tea we lie down on the katanda (bed), take out our pipes and smoke. After a smoke we take out our notebooks and make a record of everything we had found out on the road. That would probably take an hour or half an hour, and it is hard work.'

I know what he meant. When people learn I am a writer, and that I spend much of the day drinking gallons of tea, smoking roll-ups, and scribbling in my notebook, they say: 'Ooooh, it's alright for some!' But it is hard, hellish work – and what credit or sympathy do I get for this satanic slavery? None whatsoever. So spare a thought, please.

When I found a café, I treated myself to a Full English Breakfast, the sort that I imagined Stanley had consumed, just prior to setting off in search of Dr Livingstone and I asked the proprietor to fill up my flask for the arduous journey, in anticipation of my reaching Airmyn, then doubling-back along the Aire.

I looked around the cafe. A young girl was continuously and incessantly banging her cutlery on the table. Her parents were laughing, obviously proud that she had learned how to do this, and not the least bit bothered it was piddling everyone off.

As I ate my breakfast, I observed an argument brewing. A young boy, presumably the proprietor's son, was pleading for some extra pocket money, but his father was having none of it.

He turned to me, with a threatening look, and said: 'Now, don't you give him any money, either.'

I laughed and said I had no intention, to which he grimaced and returned to the kitchen.

At this, the lad looked even glummer.

Remembering how my uncle often slipped me a pound or two behind my parents' backs, I popped a couple of pound coins in his hand, and his face lit up immediately.

'Oooh, thanks mister!' he said.

'Now, don't tell your dad,' I said, with a smile, 'Or I'll be in *serious* trouble.'

The lad's smile evaporated and he held out his other hand.

'It'll cost you more than that, mister. Silence doesn't come cheap.'

I hurried back to the bus stop and fifteen minutes into the journey, the driver dropped me off at the bypass, which strides over the motorway, and advised me to walk down a slip road with no footpath, bordering farm fields, past Airmyn recycling centre, and into the village. The population of the village was recorded as 800 in 2006, which seems far too small, as Airmyn appears to be a very large village, and I would have expected a least a couple of thousand residents here. In the eighteenth century, Airmyn was a small port and people who died here would be transported by boat up the river to be buried at neighbouring village Snaith, since it was quicker to go on Aire, than by road on horse and cart.

I asked a local man for the way to Newland, on my planned trek through the villages back to Knottingley, and he pointed out the riverbank. The day was getting colder, with a damp chill in the air and a mist descending over the water. I had been travelling on bus and train since six-thirty that morning – over four hours ago – and was absolutely pooped. I had travelled all this way, over all this time, and yet this part of the expedition had only just begun. According to my map, it was about ten miles from

Airmyn to Knottingley, passing through Newland, Raith, Gowdall, Beal, Chapel Haddesley, West Haddesley and Temple Hirst.

I looked at the barren landscape towards Newland. No doubt a tempting route in summer. A tranquil and idyllic stroll. A perfect route for a sunny jaunt. But in late winter, it seemed a flat and featureless nowhere. The forbidden river of no return. The water that time forgot. And at that very point, I felt all the energy and stamina, which I had exploited on my expedition, suddenly drain from me.

And at that moment I decided to quit. Finish forever. I felt I could do no more. Couldn't be bothered to do more. Not that day. Not *any* day. So, there and then, I opted out. This was the end of the road – or river.

When the realisation dawned on me, when I decided to let myself off the hook, a whole weight seemed to flap off my shoulders and take to the air. It was not until then that I realised how this expedition jobby had taken its toll. The stops and starts. The mad dashes and dashed hopes. For every place I managed to reach, there were always two or three others I had missed. Plus other places I *had* reached, offering me no way to access the next place.

There were previous times on this expedition where I had considered throwing in the towel, giving up the goose, attempting another journey instead, and therefore another book. Whatever I plan to do, there is always a book in it somewhere. I would write a book about eating biscuits or lying in the bath if I thought anyone would read it. I had ideas for many of them, each along a Yorkshire river and each with a catchy title: *Cruise on the Ouse, Crawl along the Calder, Dawdle on the Derwent, Wander on the Wharfe*. But if I had given up on this one, would I also have given up on any of the others, as soon as I hit a snag? Probably.

It had brought to my mind a quote by Robert M. Pirsig, author of *Zen and the Art of Motorcycle Maintenance*, which read: 'I don't want to hurry it. That itself is a poisonous twentieth-century attitude. When you want to hurry something that means you no longer care about it. And want to get on to other things.' Very true. So I stuck with *Walking On Aire* – and it paid off.

Though while these wise words had encouraged me to continue on previous stretches, with obstacles encountered magically transformed into challenges, it no longer applied. It was different now. It's not like I had given up after a fortnight. In fact, on reading this book, you may get the impression that I completed this expedition over a few weeks, but it had actually taken me around eighteen months, from that very first day at Malham Tarn. That's right. *Eighteen months.* That's one-and-a-half years of wandering, meandering, shuffling and traipsing backwards, forwards, sideways, diagonally, back-to-front, upside down and inside out. I had still fared better than Marco Polo. He had set off to explore Asia – and returned no less than twenty-four years later! But still. Eighteen months is eighteen months. Still a long, long time to trek a river of seventy odd miles. But now it was time to call it a day, hang up my boots, finish my book, and think about the next expedition. If I wanted another one.

My quest had been piddled with problems from start to finish. No matter how many places I visited, there always seemed to be others I had somehow missed. In his book *Yorkshire's River Aire*, John Ogden didn't mention any times when the route may have been blocked, forcing him to retread his steps, leave the river, and seek alternative routes. Maybe there weren't any such occasions. His book was published in 1976, so his own journey would probably have been in the previous year. It was now January 2010. Places can change enormously in thirty-five years. Land could be bought and fenced off. Buildings constructed, blocking off routes. Public highways became private roads. Country lanes transformed into B-roads, then A-roads, bypasses and dual carriageways, all in a relatively short time.

My own journey had often seemed never-ending. The more research I did, and the more maps I consulted, the more and more places I discovered I had not visited. In addition to the six or so villages between Knottingley and Airmyn, I had not spent long exploring Gargrave, so I would have needed to return there.

Then there was Leeds city centre and its various tourist attractions including Teltley's Brewery Centre and the Thackeray Medical Museum and the Royal Armouries. There was Fairburn Ings nature reserve, which wasn't even on my map, which I had only discovered *after* I had passed by it, plus the multitude of suburbs around Leeds and Bradford, plus the neighbouring villages of Skipton and other towns, and the various other stretches of river that I could not access on foot. I had compiled a checklist of places, ticking off each one as I passed through, but there were always huge gaps and question marks in-between, with incredulous comments like: 'How do I get *there*?' 'How did I manage to miss *that*?' I often wondered if some of these places actually existed. If some mischievous cartographer had got bored at the office one day and started making up destinations for the sake of it. Were there *really* places called Bell Busk and Coniston Cold, or was someone just having a giggle? If someone was – it certainly wasn't me.

I had missed many of these destinations, while others I simply could not reach. With no car (getting about in this country without a vehicle is a pig at the best of times) and wholly reliant on buses, trains and aching feet, not to mention the various landowners prohibiting access to hapless hikers, hindered my expedition, together with my poor organisational and planning skills, inept map-reading, failing sunlight, strange mists and cold spots which swoop down like vultures and snatch your enthusiasm, plus attempts to hurry my progress in a bid to catch the last bus or train, or else passing right through somewhere without taking ample notice of my surroundings.

But there must have been stretches of the Congo, Nile, Ganges, Amazon, which goosed even the most hardy of explorers. Places where even gorillas and alligators and tigers wilfully avoided, making feeble excuses, opting for wide detours, chickening out, and I could empathise.

Sometimes, I had refused to get disheartened by Private Property/No Access signs, then sneaking over fences, through private woods, only to emerge hours later, thorns stuck in my hands, blood dribbling from superficial wounds, a startled squirrel clung to my head, only half the man I used to be, half-mad, half-delirious, grumbling and grunting like a Stone-Age Neanderthal, a wild man of the woods, only to scare the bejesus out of some God-fearing family out on a country amble.

I could spend another whole year dutifully following river banks which led to everywhere that I didn't want to go, and nowhere that I did, then resort to finding bus services which would take me to the places I had missed. But for what purpose? Did I really need to pass through *every* single point on a route? How many more featureless suburbs, forgotten villages, and stretches of river, so unremarkable that they don't even have place names, dotted in between all the destinations, did I need to wander along and trudge through, to prove myself a true explorer? I had set off in a spirit of adventure and discovery and had achieved just that. And so Airmyn really was the end of the road.

I have walked the River Aire, I said to myself. Then I said it again for emphasis. *I have walked the River Aire!* I may not have walked *all* of it, or seen *all* of the places, and so what if I had missed a few bits in-between? Again I pitied the writers of travel guidebooks, in their no-holds-barred, no-stones-unturned habit of seeing and doing everything, going and writing about everywhere, and I did not yearn to be ranked amongst them. I had done what I set out to do. I had walked on Aire and had now reached the end.

Chapter Nine

But not quite.

There was still that final distance to go. So, with the end in sight, which I knew I was destined to witness that very day, I climbed the stone steps and strolled along the top of a grassy knoll, the sort I imagined Lee Harvey Oswald crouched upon with his high-powered rifle, taking aim at President Kennedy, just seconds before the FBI beat him to it, and I made my way along it, dodging the benches placed at regular intervals along the path.

The riverbanks at Airmyn were lined with mudflats, and the river was wider than on most stretches. As I walked along the track, admiring the lovely houses in this pleasant village – at first glance it seemed far too large to be described as a village – I noticed a prominent building up ahead. A clock tower, which I took to be a church tower, was standing on a small green with neat gardens and benches, on a raised level, a few feet above the corner of the road. I made a note of the engraving on the tower which read: 'George Earl of Beverley 1865'. On the front of another building, just a few feet away, an inscription read: 'Sunday school erected by the right honourable, the Earl of Beverley 1834'. Next to the tower was a flagpole, with a Union Jack flapping in the wind, which could have been hoisted especially for me, to symbolically mark the end of the expedition, as if the village residents had somehow caught wind of my decision to quit the journey here, and lay on a welcoming party to mark the occasion. Perhaps there was a mayor and brass band and a sumptuous buffet round the next corner, but as I reached the clock tower and peered down the adjoining street, it was empty. But what had I been expecting? A festival, fiesta, fanfare or fandango? The Union Jack would do me.

I made a note of the time and date: 10.50am on 27th January 2010, marking the (almost) official end of the expedition. But there was still some distance to go – perhaps another half mile, so I clambered over a couple of stiles, and continued on the path to the end of the river.

I walked along another muddy track, skirting a huge farmer's field, the size of several soccer pitches, then, as the path turned right, I bore straight forward through a clump of bushes, still following the contours of the river, as the waters gushed headlong into the distance, as if hurrying to their natural end. I shared their excitement, as the end of my trip drew nearer. I turned onto an even smaller path, set on a precariously thin grass mound.

On the left, was the river battling onwards. On the right, suddenly, was an area of dense undergrowth, which I can best describe as 'misty murk', full of thick trees, deformed and hideous, but in a pleasing and thrilling sort of way. Rotting tree-trunks and branches overhung a small stream ending in a dead pool at a dead-end. It looked like a creek – the proverbial creek you could get stuck up – without a paddle. The sort where Scooby Doo and his chums always head for in the Mystery Machine.

Just then, something squelched under my foot. I just hoped it wasn't an innocent animal. It wasn't. It was a – how can I put it – innocent animal's biological deposit. Or at least I think it came from an animal. It was either a very big animal or…

I consulted my wildlife booklet, vainly searching for a section on 'identifying animal deposits', but found instead another entry entitled: 'Be Kind to the Countryside'. It read:

> *'…don't leave litter to spoil it for others. If you must use a radio keep the volume low. Respect your surroundings. Don't pick wild flowers, damage trees, rob birds' nests, or harm the wild creatures.'*

Yes. And I could add one more.

Don't let your dog or child (or nutty uncle) crap in the bushes.

I trudged on further, climbing over smaller trees, which lie in my path. As the track veered right, I came upon a clearing, where I could see the two rivers: the Aire from my left curving towards me, and the Ouse round a corner, in the channel up ahead, racing towards me. This was the end. The final few steps of an eighteen-month trek.

On reaching the Atlantic Coast, David Livingstone wrote: '…all at once the world said to us, I am finished; there is no more of me.' And I felt that the Aire was whispering similar sentiments to me.

As the currents of both rivers flowed forward, they instantly collided, doubled back and then, as if confused, spun in circles, forming cylindrical ripples like mini whirlpools at the confluence, at least twenty in total, revolving at speed, like plates on sticks, whizzing round, and yet all in virtual silence. This conjoining of waterscapes contained none of the features which prompt loud splashings. No weirs or waterfalls. No commotion at all. And no people here to witness the spectacle.

Who, in history, could have been blessed with a sight such as this? When Nelson or Columbus or Captain Cook stepped straight off their vessels and into the limelight, to deliver some sanctimonious drivel about man and destiny and soul and spirit, would they have been rewarded with such a pleasing view? They probably didn't care, having stepped into the record books and onto the gravy train for the rest of their days.

So the Aire starts seventy miles and almost two years away, at remote, solitary and isolated Malham Tarn – then ends here just past Airmyn, likewise remote, solitary and isolated.

If you can call silent and gushing water – surrounded by deserted riverbanks and extensive mudflats – beautiful, then it certainly was, but the scene and location could quite easily be overlooked. The final destination of the River Aire was quiet, tranquil, pretty – not in the way that a grass meadow is pretty at the height of summer, with its blooming daisies, wafting in the gentle breeze, certainly not as attractive as that, certainly not a high point for the tourist board to promote, but I stood there for what must have been twenty minutes, taking it in. I was completely alone. No tourists, no buildings or landmarks – other than some ugly cooling towers in the distance – to bear witness to this spectacle: the fusion of these two liquid arteries of the county. I didn't have a camera. I didn't want one. Snapshots and holiday pics serve only as brief reminders of times past, memory joggers of good times, and I knew no photo could ever portray atmosphere and emotion. And what I perceived to be a soulful place may look quite different on celluloid – a dank, doleful backwater, outside of the last village, forlorn and forgotten, conveniently nudged out of view. But for me, it was good to be there.

And I made the most of it, for I knew I would never return, with so many other places to see on this wondrous spinning globe, with so little time, and life so short. I had done what I could, and now it was time to move on. I made a sigh, took one last look at the spectacle and followed the track through this strange creek, away from the Aire, beside the Ouse, and continued along it searching for a way back to the main road. Two miles, and some busy traffic later, I was back in Goole.

And that, my friends, is where it ends.

So I was never going to pass through the villages between Knottingley and Airmyn, and discover anything about them. I would never know for sure if there was a chapel at Chapel Haddesley or a temple at Temple Hirst. Likewise, the topography and history of Gowdall, Beal, Newland and Rawcliffe were destined to remain mysteries – unexplored and uncharted – at least to me. Legendary and mythical. Magical kingdoms like Narnia, Wonderland or Atlantis. Forever to be imagined, never to be realised. Hidden away in the broom closet of my mind. Owens Woz Not Ere.

Despite my firm decision to end the expedition, there was still a nagging voice at the back of my bonce. My internal monologue, my ever-chattering mind, flatly refused to let the matter rest.

'Do you regret missing all those places?'

'Well, not really.'

'Are you sure?'

'Yes.'

'Really sure?'

'Yes.'

'Really, really…'

'Oh shut up!'

In Henry Morton Stanley's review of his expedition to find Dr Livingstone, he wrote: "We have attacked and destroyed 28 towns, three or four score villages. Fought 32 battles on land and water. Contended with 52 falls or rapids. Constructed 30 miles of tramways through forests. Hauled our canoes and boat six miles up a mountain 1500 feet high. Lifted canoes by rough mechanical skill up gigantic boulders twenty feet high. All this since we came to the river. But God be praised, our wars and troubles are over. We have pierced the dark Continent from east to west – and traced its mightiest river to its ocean.'

This, as you can guess, made me feel like a right wuss. In fact, what had *I* achieved? If anything?

I hadn't attacked and destroyed any towns. How could this be classed as an achievement? What I had done, though, was to trace one of Yorkshire's lesser-known rivers to one of its better known. The Aire to the Ouse. It may not get the pulses racing, such as an account of an intrepid expedition along the Congo – but at least I survived to tell the tale. And that was good enough for me.

At the end of her book, *Travels in West Africa*, Mary Kingsley wrote: 'I went to West Africa to die,' alluding to her feelings after the death of her parents. 'West Africa amused me and was kind to me, and was scientifically interesting, and did not want to kill me just then.'

She returned to Britain with 65 different species of fish, and 18 different species of reptile. What had I returned with? Ten different sore toes.

But I *had* achieved something else. I had been travelling the river as a writer, in a bid to discover its identity and the part it played in the lives of the people who lived nearby. I had certainly got a sense of the Aire's character. Oh – and *what* a character! With multiple personalities, its identity had changed many times over the course of my journey, and had borne witness to all aspects of history, reflecting many different aspects of human endeavour.

The Aire has run for centuries, and probably will for centuries more. It regularly changed from inconspicuous stream to wide highway of water; slow current to high-speed torrent, and in relatively short distances. The perception of the river, too, constantly switched for those walking along it, living beside it, and those desperately trying to cross it. In the rural settings, it is viewed as part of the scenery, an inspiration for artists and photographers, an integral part of the locale, gracing thousands of souvenir postcards. But in a city or suburb, it becomes a nuisance, a pointless inconvenience, separating people from where they are, to where they want to be. But even to them, the river acts as a kind of inland resort, a makeshift seaside. For rivers are like oceans, forever flowing, forever changing. Satisfied and serene one moment, angry and tempestuous the next. Unlike stagnant canals, the sight and sound of running river water is appealing to the senses, when all else around remains static. Of course, time is constantly ticking by, as are the lives of the locals, but river water is seen to move, with the passing of time merely sensed.

And the expedition had been good for me, too, as it not only gave me a subject for a book. It also gave me something additional to do than just write, for if you are a writer, then that is your vocation, and there is often not the time nor the inclination to carve out an additional 'hobby', so the trip gave me physical, as well as mental, exercise. Other explorers, too, discovered that their journeys had given them a new lease of life; perhaps even changed it completely. The explorer Ewart Grogan, author of *The Cape to Cairo* (1902), realised that his adventures had pointed his life in a totally new direction, remarking that had it not been for his African trek he would have remained 'an aimless young man wandering around Piccadilly worrying about my tie.' He later became one of the principal figures in Kenyan politics. And, given time, I'm sure my own expedition would reap positive rewards, too.

Mary Kingsley wrote: 'I have always admired men for their strength, their courage, their enterprise, their unceasing struggle for the beyond.' Although she died in 1900 – a good sixty-seven years before I was born – I felt sure she was talking about me.

I decided that my next expedition would have to involve a stretch of water I could really rely on. Not one that would be fenced off every two miles, constantly denying me access.

And I would change my mode of propulsion, too. Swapping hiking for biking.

So I needed to head for the Yorkshire coast.

I needed *A Ride Beside the Seaside*.

Next book by Andy Owens:

Urban Slave

The world is full of crap jobs and Andy Owens has had more than his fair share, from making coat-hangers and assembling tumble-driers to packing Easter Eggs and sticking walnuts on Walnut Whips.

Urban Slave is the story of his experiences: the dead-end jobs and low pay; the under-valued people he worked alongside – and the demonic bosses who employed them.

With a style described as 'Polly Toynbee meets Bill Bryson', and mixing social comment with outrageous farce, *Urban Slave* tells how the author gamely struggled through twenty-five years in low-pay Britain.

Paperback £7.95

www.andyowensbooks.co.uk